JoANN —

THANK you for All
you Do For others
& OUR Family!

Chuck & joy Day

THE TENTH MAN:
LIVING BLACK IN BLUE

The story of one of America's first black police officers

Charles E. Day

Bloomington, IN authorHOUSE® Milton Keynes, UK

AuthorHouse™
1663 Liberty Drive, Suite 200
Bloomington, IN 47403
www.authorhouse.com
Phone: 1-800-839-8640

AuthorHouse™ UK Ltd.
500 Avebury Boulevard
Central Milton Keynes, MK9 2BE
www.authorhouse.co.uk
Phone: 08001974150

This book is a work of non-fiction. Unless otherwise noted, the author and the publisher make no explicit guarantees as to the accuracy of the information contained in this book and in some cases, names of people and places have been altered to protect their privacy.

First published by AuthorHouse 7/13/2007

ISBN: 978-1-4259-5226-6 (sc)
ISBN: 978-1-4259-5227-3 (hc)

Library of Congress Control Number: 2006907487

Printed in the United States of America
Bloomington, Indiana

This book is printed on acid-free paper.

THIS BOOK IS DEDICATED TO CAREGIVERS AND PUBLIC WORKERS WHO MAKE A DIFFERENCE BY SERVING FAMILIES, COMMUNITIES AND GOD!

IN MEMORY OF MY FATHER AND MOTHER

William James Day, Sr. and Laura Mae Day

TABLE OF CONTENTS

FIGURES

A TRIBUTE TO WILLIAM JAMES DAY (PA DAY)

By

JOSIE LEE BROWN-COUNCIL

A long-time soldier in the cause–Christ's cause. Even though you are gone, you will be remembered through each passing day. Joy, love, meekness, dedication and faithfulness to your family.

You taught us that sometimes when things seem the worst they turn out to be the best. Along life's path, you taught us that while we cannot always have our plans realized, God's plans are better. You have gone on ahead of us, but remain. You left us in his care; you have shown us that we are all a part of God and that we are always known, and that God is everywhere. The sunshine of your love will surround us always.

After your mother went home to be with the Lord, you shared the sheltered love of your aunt and uncle, Lillian and Lawrence Brown, and other members of the family. You returned such love in an unselfish way. You took the torch of love and generosity from your Aunt Lillian and Uncle Lawrence and carried it as a guidepost into your adult life. You chose Jesus as your main friend and savior at an early age.

If you could speak, you would call each of your children by name: Patsy, William, Charles, Edmund, and Robert.

You would say to them, "Love ye one another as I have loved you." You would pass the torch of love and generosity to each of them.

Your children are a tribute to you. You were one of the strongest, gentlest, proudest and kindest fathers and grandfathers in the entire world. You lived a life that will always shine within our hearts and souls. The light you gave us will be forever a lamp unto our feet and a light to our pathways.

May we imitate your life of integrity, beauty, love, sacrifice, and obedience before God.

Loving father, as we bid you adieu, may loving thoughts of you always remind us of the sweet memories of you.

PREFACE

The Tenth Man: Living Black in Blue started as an idea some four years ago. I recall visiting my older brother William (Bill) and his wife, Dorothy, in Atlanta and asking for their blessing in doing the book. I recall Bill's comment that he wanted to do the same, which gave me another level of validation that it was a good idea. My brother Robert, who still lives in Savannah, also gave me his blessing in proceeding with the project.

As it turned out, I became exceedingly busy with my management consulting practice and other community outreach programs and had to drop the book from month to month. It is also a book that is very personal, making it harder in many ways to go through the paces. Deep emotional moments caused long pauses for reflection on how others have lived their lives in a manner that has enabled me to be where I am today.

Life is not easy! I discovered a lot in researching the book about my folks, the police department, men and women who were in our lives as youngsters and those who stood up for civil rights in my hometown, Savannah, GA. I focused principally on ways that others in the African American community sacrificed many things to make it possible for so many others to progress more fully as American citizens. From literature research, personal interviews, and reading other works I captured many ideas about life in the '50s and '60s that greatly influenced me and, I expect, also influenced my brothers and others in our family.

One of the greater discoveries in the project was newly found relatives, including a grandniece and a half sister, Bettye. I met both while returning to Savannah to do research and participate in a performance with the Savannah State University Men's Glee Club Alumni. I came to peace in getting to know them late in life. Bettye was looking for closure, family ties, and acceptance. I have given both acceptance and love as I know my parents would have wanted me to.

I was introduced to my half sister, Patsy, early in life. However, I did not know her as an adult. And when she passed a few years ago, I not only mourned the loss of a family member, but the unfortunate changes in our lives that kept us apart and out of touch. It was at Patsy's funeral that we became reacquainted with her son, Lloyd, and met for the first time our grandniece, Marlo, and her mother Marie-Solange. These meetings seem to me not to be accidental, but God's way of restoring a missing link in family ties.

Having time and courage to write any book is truly a blessing! While my first book, *Call Center Operations: Profiting From Teleservices*, published by McGraw-Hill, included 500 pages of business process, management and technology documentation, it was considerably easier to write and less time consuming to actually publish. It probably helped that I was commissioned with the first book and on a relatively strict deadline.

By contrast, *The Tenth Man: Living Black in Blue* took far more thought than I ever expected with every word, chapter, photo, organization and, just as importantly, deciding if telling personal truths about so many things– as I saw them–would offend anyone, especially family members. I pray that my forthright intentions will outweigh any thought to the contrary by readers.

The delay in completing this book took me to an age beyond that of my father at his death and caused me to reflect greatly on how limited longevity was in my Daddy's era. This realization motivated me to establish an endowment fund with The Philadelphia Foundation, Inc. as a memorial to my mother and father as part of my 60th birthday celebration. Instead of gifts, family and friends helped me contribute to this fund, www.philafound. org, to provide financial assistance to ordinary youngsters seeking to go to a college in Savannah, GA and advance in criminal justice, law enforcement, nursing or a related field. These areas of study represent the professional interests of my parents. Proceeds from this book are also to be used for building the William J. and Laura M. Day Memorial Fund.

It is my hope that readers will accept these personal stories in the context of passing information on to the younger generations about family life, challenges of living and realities often out of our control as witnessed by the history of Savannah and the civil rights movement. It is intended to help families of all backgrounds give focus to similar issues in their lives. By reading these stories, if my sons and grandchildren will brace themselves, give life their all, choose to be happy, live spiritual lives, respect all peoples and with God keep family first – I will have succeeded!

ACKNOWLEDGEMENTS

I wish to acknowledge John Alliston White and David Jones who were guiding lights in their contributions to me getting started with research and giving such complete information about my Daddy, their careers as policemen with the Savannah Police Department and the ins and outs of the Savannah community that I only knew as a child. I was also honored to spend time with both W.W. Law, renowned civil rights leader and postal worker (who delivered on our block) and William Wallace, former city policeman, who both contributed to this book with exceedingly open and generous interviews. Unfortunately, both died soon after primary research was completed and before this book was published. These black American men also represent the purpose of this book with their lives and community work as a civil rights leader and a black police officer in Savannah, GA in the 1950s and '60s.

Many thanks with unconditional love to my family members who have been very supportive of this project and me personally. Thanks to Joy, William, Jr., Robert, Dorothy, Bettye, Marlo, Chip, Bobby, April, Jurnee, Justin, Daijha, Monica, Heather, William, III, Jennifer, Kristina, Davita, Aszurae, Amber, Dorian, Adriona, Tony, Loretta, Channel, Schannan, Anthony, Michael, Kelvin, Landon and Willie. Very special thanks to Josie Lee Brown-Council for writing such a wonderful tribute to my Daddy and sitting with me over genealogy charts and discussing my Daddy's family background. Thanks also to Gloria Braddy for nursing Mama when she became paralyzed.

There are those who helped me draft, edit, organize, scan photographs, complete literature research, draw sketches and just discuss things when I needed to learn, get a second opinion or just talk and vent: Sandra Bouchelion, Judith Light, Marcia Jones, Barbara Heuer, Russell Lewis, Peter Ulrich, Marge and George Stevens, Tony Oliver, Essie Nealy, Liz Blount, Ruth Mullino, Charles Elmore, Major Ralph Bashlor, Jr., Mary Ann Jones, Alex Zabrosky, Jodi Wibbels, and the Reverends Charles Hoskins and Marc Britt. The book cover painting is by Russell Lewis as well as several sketches within. Peter Ulrich painted several memorable scenes of Chippewa Square, the Talmage Bridge and Savannah's waterfront. Very special thanks to Winnie Shows for sharing her professional gift of book review and organization.

Thank you to the many organizations that helped me and people who taught, encouraged and/or attended school with me in Savannah, many with whom I have continued a relationship over five decades, from Florance Street Elementary School, Cuyler Junior High School, Paulsen Street School, Alfred E. Beach Senior High School, Savannah State University, St. Matthew's Episcopal

Church, the Alpha Phi Alpha Fraternity, the NAACP, the YMCA, Frank Callen Boys and Girls Club, the DeSoto Hilton Hotel, Savannah Yacht and Country Club, Hester's Restaurant, and Weiner Groceries. And to Willie Blount, deceased, who found work for us (while we were in school) at many places in Savannah, including beach homes and the two Socialite Christmas Parties described in Midnight in the Garden of Good and Evil by John Berendt. To Critz Buick and my Uncle Howard Watts, Sr., also deceased, for entrusting to me and college friends new Buick cars to transport between Florida, South Carolina and Savannah, GA.

I wish to acknowledge the organizations and people I continue to benefit from in my adult life as both a means of continued growth spiritually, mentally and physically including St. John's Episcopal Church – Broad Creek, Savannah State University Men's Glee Club Alumni, the Metropolitan Chorus in Washington, DC, the Fort Washington Community Chorus in Maryland, the Institute of Management Consultants, Inc., the Tantallon Golf and Country Club, the Tantallon Community Players and the Kappa Epsilon Lambda Chapter of the Alpha Phi Alpha Fraternity.

Many thanks for assistance and information to the Savannah Morning News, the Herald Newspaper, the Savannah Tribune, TravelHost, Inc. of Savannah, the

Savannah Chamber of Commerce, the Savannah Parks and Recreation Services, Telfair Museum of Arts, the Rev. Dr. Ralph Mark Gilbert Civil Rights Museum, Savannah State University, Armstrong Atlantic State University, Savannah College of Art and Design (SCAD).

The assistance from AuthorHouse Publishing Company was tremendously supportive. The upfront work and guidance by Elaine Headley-Jerome, book cover layout and project coordination by Bob DeGroff and book design layout were all done professionally, patiently and caringly given the number of changes to complete this work.

In addition to primary research assistance and willingness of many to give of their time for lengthy interviews, this book would not be possible without the cooperation, permissions, photography, and electronic imaging and prior publications by others. I also apologize in advance if through all of my efforts to be thorough, I have still missed anyone or organization who contributed.

The following works were not only sources for information, but essential in getting permission to include material herein. This is also a suggested reading list.

1. Tuck, Stephen G.N. *Beyond Atlanta: The Struggle For Racial Equality in Georgia, 1940-1980*. University of Georgia Press.
2. Baldwin, Frederick C. *...We Ain't What We Used To Be*. Telfair Academy of Arts and Sciences.

3. Elmore, Charles J. *Black America Series, Savannah, Georgia*. Arcadia Publishing.

4. Hoskins, Charles Lwanga. *Out of Yamacraw and Beyond: Discovering Black Savannah*. The Gullah Press.

5. Berendt, John. *Midnight in the Garden of Good and Evil*. Random House.

6. Piechocinski, Elizabeth Carpenter. *Once Upon An Island: The Barrier and Marsh Islands of Chatham County, Georgia*

7. Debolt, Margaret Wayt. *Savannah A Historical Portrait*. Hallmark Publishing Company.

8. Nesbit, Martha Giddens. *Savannah: Crown of the Colonial Coast*. Towery Publishing, Inc.

9. LaGrange, David. *Savannah Police Officers: Celebrating 200 Years of Service*. Turner Publishing Company

10. Dulaney, W. Marvin. *Black Police in America*. Indiana University Press.

11. Bolton Jr., Kenneth and Feagin, Joe R. *Black in Blue: African American Police Officers and Racism*. Routledge.

12. Elmore, Charles J. *First Bryan, 1788-2001: The Oldest Continuous Black Baptist Church in America*. Lewis Printing Company.

13. Hoskins, Charles Lwanga. *Yet With a Steady Beat*. The Gullah Press.

Finally, I would like to acknowledge and thank my deceased father and mother for all of their loving care, guidance, teachings and values that have molded me and my brothers to become the productive and responsible individuals we are today. May they continue to rest in peace and know that this book is being dedicated to them and to those who are caregivers and public workers who make a difference in the lives of their families and the greater community.

INTRODUCTION

This book is the life story of my father, William J. Day, Sr. (1912-1972) of Savannah, Georgia, who served from 1947 to 1972 as one of the first black police officers in the U.S. My research on my father, ironically, took interviews and reading in order to learn more about him after his death than I discovered while as a youngster growing up with him.

While the focus of this story is about a man's life, his values, family, friends, work, struggles, accomplishments and relationships, it is also about the civil rights movement and the many heroes created and recognized in the South. Finally, it is about the charm, character and style of one of the South's most remarkable cities, Savannah, which is rich in heritage and beauty.

The complexity of being a black American peacekeeper, civil rights advocate, and bearer of enormous family and financial responsibilities is unique and unlike the singular issues of most modern generation families. Or is it?

Several objectives drive my desire to document my father's life and experiences in the South. First, the book is for our family members living now and for those yet to be born. It strives to explain to the generations of the Day family and similar families what it was like to live in his time and place, the consequences of his devotions to causes, and the difficulties of managing conflicts that, in some cases, were life threatening. It also documents the many accomplishments and struggles of black police officers throughout the South and elsewhere across the United States.

PROLOGUE: 1963

Something was terribly wrong. Six squad cars had pulled up to the front of our home and Sgt. John A. White, the highest ranking black police officer in Savannah, was escorting my father, Officer William Day, to the door. Mama's face was stricken, and Daddy's was dark and unreadable. I looked at my brother, and he stared back, as worried and shocked as I was. The officers accompanying Daddy said things like, "Things will work out." "It's going to be okay." "Keep the faith," and "We will patrol regularly as long as it takes until this flies over." But not one of them explained what had happened, how it happened, and the rightness or the inappropriateness of it all.

CHAPTER 1
THE ORIGINAL NINE

Sixteen years earlier, in May 1947, Savannah made news across the United States by hiring its first black policemen, second only to Miami. In a documentary, *The Original Nine, Savannah's First Black Policemen*, confirmed that in 1947, Savannah became the second city south of the Mason-Dixon Line to hire black police officers.

After three months of secretly being trained in a Masonic Temple, a group of twenty recruits were ready for induction and service. Nine of them were sworn in on Saturday, May 3rd and introduced publicly on Sunday, May 4th at a dedication service for a new city recreation center for blacks at 37th Street and Ogeechee Road.

While the primary objective of the gathering was to dedicate the building, which was a major addition to the black community, many attended the ceremony to hear an

Original Nine Black Police Officers – Savannah, GA

address by Mayor John G. Kennedy and see Savannah's first black policemen. Several other city administration positions were also announced with the appointment of blacks. These included Alma Rivers, a cousin of mine, as the matron at city jail, a "floor walker" at city jail, assistant superintendent of recreation and playgrounds, city lot porter, assistant supervisor of recreation, and a sanitary inspector.

The chief of police at the time was James W. Rogers. A number of the black community leaders who were instrumental in the appointment of black police officers attended and participated in the program. John W. McGlockton, who was president of the Citizens Democratic Club, served as master of ceremonies. The Rev. Dr. Ralph Mark Gilbert, pastor of the First African Baptist Church and also president of the State Conference of the National Association for the Advancement of Colored People

(NAACP), commented during the ceremony that he had planned a trip to New York and "was glad that he could tell his friends there that although Herman Eugene Talmadge was in power in McRae, Mayor Kennedy presided over Savannah." The black policemen introduced publicly on May 4th, now known as the "Original Nine," included Howard J. Davis, John Alliston White, Frank B. Mullino, James Nealy, Milton Hall, William N. Malone, Leroy Wilson, Stepney Houston and Alexander Grant, Jr.

W.W. Law, who headed the NAACP, credits Rev. Dr. Ralph Mark Gilbert with community activism that led to the appointment of the nine black officers. In October 1984, Law said, "Dr. Gilbert was perhaps the most exceptional

Police Chief James W. Rogers 1947-1948

black man in this community in this century. He made contributions in every facet of community life. He was the black chairman of the Community Chest and the black chairman of the Christmas Seals. He mobilized black religious leaders to support the effort to form the Greenbriar Children's Center and led the effort to create the West Broad YMCA-USO with the idea that after the war it would be our colored Y."

Law goes on in that address to honor the retirement of Lt. John A. White, an original black police officer, and to credit John W. McGlockton, who headed a joint political action committee composed of the Negro Voters League, the Elks, the NAACP, and an organization called the HUB. Mr. Law also credits John Q. Jefferson, Dr. J.W. Jamerson, Jr., and Ms. Metella W. Maree, who was at the Paulson School as a teacher and headed a NAACP committee on voter education.

At the time of this writing, all but two of the Original Nine are deceased. Lt. John Allison White is approaching eighty years of age and enjoys a life of retirement and participation in community affairs and works occasionally at the Savannah waterfront. He is an avid checker board player at the Savannah Checker Club on Martin Luther King, Jr. Boulevard and 37th Street. White was on the police force for some thirty-eight years after serving in the Marine Corps with the rank of corporal, being a military policeman and one of the first blacks to serve in combat in the Marines.

In June 1947, the *New York Times* published a special "Outsider Report" by reporter John N. Popham:

Nine Negro policemen, the first ever appointed in Georgia, have been patrolling their beats here for the past six weeks. Against a turbulence of statewide political conflict on the issue of white supremacy, the Savannah experiment in bettering communal race relations has progressed so satisfactorily that its opponents now largely concede that Negro policemen are here to stay.

Popham also pointed out that the appointment of these men stemmed from a desire to improve law enforcement in the black section of the community as well as to recognize the right of blacks to vote in primary election campaigns. He further explained that the experiment in Chatham County, which includes Savannah, was one of the heavily populated urban counties to support Eugene Talmadge, who campaigned for governor on a white supremacy platform. The Citizens Progressive League garnered the credit for turning out black voters in Savannah's municipal elections, accounting for about one-third of the votes. This alone assured representation in city government.

Popham also mentioned that even though the son of the late governor, Herman Talmadge, felt that no white primary measure could be drawn that would be upheld by federal courts and that Negro voting in a primary election must be taken into consideration for the future. This was a signal that appointments of blacks in municipal positions were a must.

Original Black Police Officers at Headquarters

Howard J. Davis later became the first county police officer in Chatham County, Georgia. He was first recruited to the Savannah Police Department after serving a tour in the U.S. Army as a military policeman. Frank B. Mullino left the Savannah Police Force after several years and became a Merchant Mariner, which was a very lucrative occupation in Savannah, especially in the 1950s. Mullino served in the Army before joining the police force and was also believed to have military police experience.

James Nealy served as my father's partner for years on the force and retired with great honors after twenty-five years of service. The Nealys were also godparents to my younger brother, Robert Arthur. Nealy himself was in the

U.S. Army as a military policeman before being recruited to the Original Nine in 1947.

Milton Hall was one of the most colorful Original Nine members with his great dancing ability and his shiny motorcycle, which was uncommon among blacks in the late '40s and '50s. Milton left the force after three years and formed the successful Milton Taxi Cab Company. In 1954, he competed in Pennsylvania at Landstown Motorways on his bike.

William N. Malone is the second of the two remaining Original Nine who lives in Savannah. Unfortunately he is suffering from Alzheimer's disease and was unavailable for interview with this work. Malone served in the U.S. Army before joining the Savannah Police Department and worked thirty years as a policeman before retirement and illness.

Leroy Wilson served eight years as an Original Nine police officer and left the force to pursue a career in real estate in the Savannah area.

Stepney Houston left the force after four years and established residence in the state of Virginia and became a residential and commercial painter. Houston's background included the armed services in the Savannah area before joining as a member of the Original Nine.

Alexander Grant, Jr. was dismissed from the force in controversy after three weeks with the Savannah Police Department and went on to become a successful electrician in the Savannah area. He is still alive and revered by his family for being one of the Original Nine.

CHAPTER 2
THE TENTH MAN

My father was the tenth man.

On May 29, 1947 the *Savannah Tribune* included an article about the addition of William J. Day as the tenth black policeman to be hired by Savannah. The article was entitled, "Day Succeeds Grant as City Policeman."

> A new Negro city policeman, William J. Day, was sworn in Tuesday at the City Hall to succeed Alexander Grant, Jr. who was dismissed from the force this Saturday. Grant, who was one of the nine Negro policemen appointed to the force several weeks ago, was discharged from the service for 'falsifying records.' It is claimed that fingerprint records from the Federal Bureau of Investigation showed that Grant had once been arrested in con-

nection with bootleg whiskey operations, whereas Grant claimed on his application that there was no police record connected with his name. Chief Rogers, chief of Savannah Police Department, said that Grant had made a good record since his appointment to the force. Officer Day, who succeeds Grant, has been employed as a truant officer for the Board of Education and also drives a school bus.

What was not discussed in the Tribune was that Alexander Grant was a young boy and a minor at the time he was arrested with his father and others and had no idea about the legality of the family's sideline.

Officer William Day as Young Recruit

The *New York Times* article by John N. Popham dated June 25, 1947, included praise by the community regarding the addition of Negro policemen. Judge Emmanuel Lewis of the Recorders Court, one of the organizers of the Citizens Progressive League, estimated that by June the Negro patrolmen had brought some fifty cases before him. He mentioned that the Negro policemen wore their uniforms in court, which contradicted other accounts. Their presentation of evidence had been on par with that of any rookie policeman, according to Judge Lewis, who commended one of them for excellent police work and preventing a domestic quarrel from developing into an injury or death.

The Rev. Dr. Ralph Mark Gilbert, pastor of the First African Baptist Church and President of the State Conference for the National Association for the Advancement of Colored People, said, "Reaction to the patrolmen among white and Negro residents had been very fine."

"There has been a sense of belonging to the community for Negroes," he said. "It has resulted in pride and citizenship and real interest in civic life. You could see it at once in precinct meetings we hold."

The *New York Times* went on to acknowledge the appointment of William J. Day as the tenth Negro policeman appointed.

One of the Negro policemen, William J. Day, thirty-five years old, father of two children and a graduate of Georgia State College, said that "people here have treated us just swell."

Officer Day said that "several of the policemen have been commended for good work" and that he "believes several crimes have been prevented because "people seek us out." Day also said that "white store keepers in the Negro section have ex-pressed satisfaction." The Negro policemen receive $170.00 a month. They work eight hours a day with a day off plus an extra day off when they switch from night to day duty."

The life of a Negro policeman in the late '40s and '50s was not easy. Fifty years later, John A. White, one of the original nine black officers, would comment, "I've been shot at so many times, it's not funny."

David Jones, a former City Alderman and retired Savannah police officer, commented on the "community-oriented policing" which took a gentler approach. "We knew everyone," he said, "and you can solve a lot of crimes by getting to know people." Jones said that in one case he was handed a scribbled note from a woman with an indication of a tip about a moonshine still, which resulted in one of the officer's biggest illegal liquor busts.

The process for selecting black candidates for police work began several months before May 3, 1947. Approximately sixty candidates were considered based on their character, literacy, and military experience. Sixteen of them, including

William J. Day, were secretly trained without pay in the fundamentals of police work. The meetings were held twice weekly for two and a half months at a Masonic Hall in the black community where they received basic training and possibly even more in-depth training than their white counterparts.

Hiring black policemen was both symbolic and practical for black community leaders, lowering an important and highly visible barrier to black progress. These assignments were considered pivotal. Along with the other city positions filled with blacks, this began establishing a pattern for other gains.

CHAPTER 3
"PA" DAY

William J. Day was born in Waycross, Georgia on June 12, 1912. His mother was Mattie Day. Mattie had four siblings: Rachel, Elizabeth, John and James (Shing). Their parents were Willie and Phyllis Young.

William Day's upbringing and the roots of this police officer make a fascinating story in itself. It is the story of an African American family and the ties that made "family" so special and influential. Early childhood uncertainties, being cared for by relatives instead of parents are enough to bring down self-confidence and assertiveness of many. But not so for "Pa" Day. That's what this young trooper was called. This is how he was known by family members. He took on many jobs and responsibilities at an early age and took care of older relatives. It served as a genuine test of what was to come later. To get a handle on the vague history of

"Pa" Day in Civilian Suit

the early years, Josie Lee Brown-Council, a senior cousin, recalls Pa Day's early years and development. Here is what she says:

"From the outset, it was apparent God had blessed William with special gifts of loveliness, talent, intelligence, and the most priceless gift of all, a shining warmth and ability to love and be loved by all who came within his presence.

"Early in life he realized the need to help and guide his life's journey. Thereby, he confessed to Christ and became a devout member and dedicated worker at Second Arnold Baptist Church, where he served in several capacities of leadership, mainly on the usher board and hospitality club.

"He received his early education at the public schools in Chatham County and completed his high school education at Cuyler Street School. His college work was done at Georgia State College (now Savannah State University), where he obtained an excellent scholastic record.

"Everybody close to him in the family called him Pa Day, and mother Rachel called him "You Par." No one ever called him Mr. Day, but to the literally hundreds of Savannahians who knew him, he was simply known as Pa Day. People referred to him in that manner out of respect more than anything else. He was a policeman and educator for more than twenty years. He was an integral part of Haven Home School under the leadership of Mrs. Ophelia McIver. He transported students to the school while matriculating at Georgia State College. He was highly respected by students and policemen, as well as in the community."

Josie Lee continues, "Pa Day's works and deeds earned him much acclaim. He has been my hero and the perfect role model, loving and sharing so much. When I think of

Pa Day, I am reminded of these words by Robert Louis Stevenson:

"That man is a success who has lived well, laughed often and loved much; who has gained the respect of intelligent men and love of children; who has filled his niche and accomplished his task; who leaves the world better than he found it, whether by an improved poppy, a perfect poem or a rescued soul; who never lacked appreciation of earth's beauty or failed to express it; who looked for the best in others and gave the best he had."

Josie Lee says further, "These words are descriptive to a large degree of the life and work of William James Day, Sr. because he was a man of large intellect, spiritual and social gifts, who gave freely of himself to his family, his wife, his children, and to those whom he served throughout the United States."

Because he was born into a relatively struggling family situation, and raised by a single parent (his mother), he did not have much information about his father. His mother died when he was nearly a teenager. The loss must have been truly traumatic for Pa Day, the kid.

Daddy suffered acute problems with his feet in the early days. He had operations and had to use crutches, which affected him in his teen years the way some kids may have been affected by polio, which must have been an additional hardship. It is ironic that after a dozen transitional jobs and occupations, he would ultimately end up as a foot soldier or patrolman walking a beat. It is my guess that his nickname, Pa Day, represented the self-confidence and courage that he must have mustered to fend off all of the worries and challenges, showing his family and the world that he could grow up to be a responsible adult and man.

Many in Savannah recall his living on the east side of town with his Aunt Rachel Day on Anderson Street, where they both attended the Second Arnold Baptist Church. While Aunt Rachel was his guardian after his mother, Mattie's death, their roles reversed in his late teen years so that it became imperative that Pa Day was gainfully employed and capable of supporting his aunt, whom he had grown to love just as his mother.

The list of jobs my father had assumed before becoming a police officer in 1947 is truly amazing. These included working as a National Biscuit Company truck driver, a barber, a projectionist at the Star Theater, a Pullman porter, a truant officer, a school bus driver, a teacher, and finally in 1946—a cadet for the Savannah Police Department.

It is striking that with the many challenges of hanging on to family at a young age, how aunts, uncles and cousins played important roles in building family and keeping family values intact. After both a mother and an aunt passing on, Pa Day became solidly integrated into the Brown family headed by Grand Uncle and Aunt Lawrence

Lawrence and Lillian Brown's 50th Wedding Anniversary

and Lillian Brown. There were some eight cousins allowing him to draw close: Homer, Roscoe, Agnes, Alvenia, Josie Lee, Estella Marie, Marco, and Lawrence, Jr. It also helped that Uncle Lawrence Brown lived just around the corner from where the Day family ultimately lived on Burroughs Street. All of the big family to-dos were held at Uncle Lawrence and Aunt Lillian Brown's home on West 39th Street, where Christmas and other holidays took on a very special meaning. It was the only family that I knew that could muster up some sixty people for the fiftieth wedding anniversary of Lawrence and Lillian Brown, Sr.

While the Browns' support was crucial to maintaining some semblance of family structure for Pa Day, it was also immensely important to his children. Lawrence Brown, Sr. was like a grandfather to my brothers and me. Prior to receiving our first black and white TV in 1957, we would go around the corner to his house to watch the fights. He was an avid boxing fan, and it was a favorite spot to huddle. Uncle Lawrence would weave a commentary through all the competitors' blows with the enthusiasm and vigor of a man much younger than his seventy plus years. It is abundantly clear to me as I write this book how important family linkages have become—first as a child and again as a father of two sons and now with grandchildren. The duality of extended families through both parents adds significantly to a feeling of well being from the love and caring of others.

Early jobs and responsibility for Pa Day were not only for development of experience at skills, but an absolute necessity in providing for a family's well being. This experience early on causes a person to grow up fast and in a mature manner. I believe my father was also bestowed with the title "Pa Day" because of his demonstration of maturity and early responsibility. In other words, he took care of business.

The early years did indeed serve as a stringent test for what was to come for Pa Day. These many jobs dealing with all types of people and different situations and taking responsibility within public contact positions were a strong foundation, and my father accomplished even more.

He received a degree in sociology science from Savannah State University (formerly Georgia State College) in 1944 (the year I was born)—an almost unbelievable accomplishment for anyone in those days and especially a black man. All this experience and education in life and school qualified him to take and pass a test and be considered as part of the initial twenty recruits for the Savannah City Police Department. He was off and running and his life would never be the same!

CHAPTER 4
SAVANNAH

There are many descriptions of Savannah from a tourist and visitor point of view, but for those born and raised in the southern tradition of this port city and who lived on the "the other side of the tracks," life's perspective is slightly different. What is not different is a deep appreciation of being alive in a magnificent city, overall, to raise a family and enjoy the natural beauty of America's First Planned City.

Savannah's history stands out and includes a different kind of respect for the many street squares, Broughton Street, General Oglethorpe, Sherman's march to the sea, close proximity to Defuskie Island, Ft. Pulaski, Hunter's Air Field, and Fort Screven. Notable industries include Union Bag Paper Company, longshoremen, Savannah Sugar Refinery, Grumman Aircraft, and Great Dane Trailers.

Chippewa Square

Savannah was at that time the land of opportunity and transition for black Americans working for the government. Two of my classmates, Floyd Adams from high school and Otis Johnson from college, have actually been elected to city government. Floyd Adams became Savannah's first black mayor, and Otis Johnson followed him—a phenomenal tale and history of events.

Interestingly, slaves were initially banned in Georgia. However, it is believed that they were borrowed as day laborers with permission of the government of South Carolina. The day laborers assisted with common chores, running sawmills and teaching settlers the skills for building houses. The labor laws were modified in the early 1750s, and by early 1770 there were some twelve to thirteen thousand slaves in Georgia with many being brought from West Africa, including African Gullah from Sierra Leone. Some influence of the importation of Gullah people is still linked with nearby Defuskie, South Carolina and on the Sapelo Islands.

John Wesley, founder of Methodism in England, arrived in Georgia and delivered his first sermon in 1736 in what is now Christ Church often referred to "the Mother Church of Georgia." Wesley is credited with the founding of the Savannah Sunday School. Wesley's brother, Charles, served as Secretary for Indian Affairs in Georgia and personal assistant to James Oglethorpe, European founder of Savannah, who is said to have attended Christ Episcopal Church on St. Simon's Island when John Wesley delivered his first sermon.

In later years, approximately 1793, Eli Whitney is credited with the development of the first commercial cotton gin on the Mulberry Plantation some ten to twelve miles outside of Savannah.

During the American Revolution, the British took over Savannah on December 29, 1778, and held it until July 1782. A land/sea force of French and Americans tried to retake the city in 1779 first by siege and then by direct assault but failed dismally. Savannah was the state capital from 1782 to 1785.

Following the Civil War, blacks acquired voting rights to participate more in the political process. Some were even elected to the Georgia State Legislature as early as 1868. The political power of blacks waned when troops from the north left the south. This resulted in the dominant power structure reneging on the promise that forty acres and a mule would be set aside for each black family. It would seem like an eternity for blacks to achieve full equality and representation in government.

With the growth in trade, and especially after the invention of the cotton gin and the construction of railroads extending to cotton fields throughout central Georgia, Savannah became a rival to Charleston, South Carolina, as a commercial center. The first steamship to cross the Atlantic, the S.S. Savannah, left this Georgia port for Liverpool in 1819. The Civil War brought a disastrous turn of events in Savannah in 1862 when nearby Ft. Pulaski fell to Union troops. Savannah was blockaded. The city did not fall until December 1864. William Tecumseh Sherman launched a successful "Atlanta campaign" as general of the Union Army. In November 1864 he set fire to Atlanta and subsequently began his march through Georgia to the Atlantic Ocean, culminating in December in Savannah while leaving in its path a scene of great destruction. In

May 1864, Sherman, with some 62,000 men, 2,500 wagons and 3,500 horses, mules and camels began his infamous "march to the sea." In late December 1864, his troops entered Savannah, The opposition surrendered quite easily and without a major fight.

Sherman did not burn Savannah, but reportedly telegraphed President Lincoln indicating he had captured Savannah as a Christmas gift while obtaining great supplies, ammunition and thousands of bales of cotton.

By the end of 1867 the blockade was over, and the city began to rebuild its most lucrative industry, shipping. Auctions for cotton and other commodities took place on Factor's Walk and the city became once again active in business and commerce.

In the late 1880s, Savannah was operating at its shipping peak with more than two billion bales of cotton yearly and on almost 2,000 vessels. At the turn of the century, however, Savannah was impacted by an economic downturn. Cotton production went up, but prices were down. Land began to be developed for commercial use. The emergence of the boll weevil, a beetle insect of Mexican descent, which damages cotton buds and limits growth, left Savannah's cotton enterprise on a downslide. Overall, the cotton industry declined by two-thirds. Ironically, the disaster from the cotton industry stimulated interest in mimicking cities throughout the southeast where other industries and enterprises began to be developed. The Savannah Sugar Refinery, now Savannah Foods and Industries, began operation in the city in 1917. In 1937, Union Bag, now Union Camp, a Kraft paper bag manufacturing company, also constructed a factory in Savannah. The two companies offered an economic base in manufacturing that provided new products to be shipped through Savannah ports, which boosted the economy as well. Ship building became a major factor in Savannah's recovery where some 2,400 Liberty ships, nicknamed Ugly Ducklings, were built to transport soldiers and cargo during World War II and into the Vietnam War.

One of the most nationally known and recognized landmarks in Savannah is the home of Juliette Gordon Low, also known as Daisy, who was born in 1860, daughter of Nellie Kinzie and William Washington Gordon, II, a cotton trader whose father built the Central of Georgia Railroad. She formed the Girl Scouts of America in March 1912, with two patrol groups referred to as Girl Guides. The Girl Scout movement has been always inclusive. There is evidence indicating that the organization did have members of different racial and ethnic groups early in history. The 1912 preamble to the Constitution of Girl Scouts of the USA says, "We affirm that the Girl Scout movement shall be open to all girls and adults who accept the Girl Scout Promise and Law." Juliette Gordon Low declared that indeed the

Girl Scout program was designed "for all the girls." Girl Scouts now number more than 50 million girls and young women across the country.

Savannahians are also quite proud of Johnny Mercer, a native and Academy Award winner for his hit "Moon River" from the film, *Breakfast at Tiffany's* in 1962 and for "Days of Wine of Roses," a theme song for the 1963 movie bearing the same name. Mercer died in 1976 and is buried at the Bonaventure Cemetery. His former home within the city was the subject of John Berendt's book, *Midnight in the Garden of Good and Evil.*

A rare distinction of an American city like Savannah is its involvement in so many faces of a nation. Savannah has played a role in early U.S. history, to the Civil War, through the country's agricultural development, international trade, the civil rights movement, architecture, state and specialty schools for higher education, landscape, beaches, fishing and water sports, industries and industrialization. The city also has been involved in the nation's military deployments from early times to current wars, cultural diversity, shared participation in government, suburban sprawl, inner city trials and tribulations, and more.

Savannah is not a perfect model for an untroubled city. It is not without problems and challenges. It struggles to restore deteriorating housing, maintain jobs, eliminate the effect of drugs and crime, and assure that all children succeed in education, house the homeless, feed the hungry, and retain the best and brightest to govern with vision and keep tranquility. What is most relevant is the remarkable progress of a city ruled by Jim Crow laws, during my lifetime, progressing over time with its defining qualities of grace and beauty to become an even more unique and attractive city–Savannah!

CHAPTER 5
LIFE IN BLUE

The new officers patrolled the predominantly black areas of Savannah along West Broad Street (now Martin Luther King, Jr. Boulevard) from the Union Station to Henry Street. These officers did not patrol white areas of the city, nor were they permitted to arrest white offenders. One police officer was eventually assigned to patrol the black portion of East Broad Street, which was way across town. These first black policemen were asked not to wear their uniforms while shopping off duty on the city's main street so that the "political enemies" could not start rumors that Negro policemen were patrolling in white areas.

The officers also were instructed that they could only arrest white people in the Negro section if a violation was of an "emergency nature." If it concerned a developing

Officers Make Donation to Greenbriar Children's Center

incident, they were to "summon radio cars manned by white policemen."

Makeshift barracks, a substation, were officially designated and named Precinct No. 9. It was located on Waldburg Street between West Broad and Burroughs Streets. Lockers were installed to permit officers to change out of their uniforms before they went off duty. The black officers were required to store their uniforms, badges and revolvers in the lockers when not on duty to avoid having uniformed black police officers passing through white areas on their way to and from work. Some officers indicated that initially they also were not permitted to wear their uniforms when appearing in court.

In addition to the normal stress associated with police work, the original black policemen faced racial discrimination even from within the department. The late

Lt. William (Billy) E. Wallace recounted in an interview on March 21, 2002, that in the early days when black police officers were permitted to use police cars, white policemen would actually blow the seats off with air hoses before sitting in the same car on shift change. Wallace said it was their objective to do it in a manner for blacks to see. Wallace went on to comment that because of William Day's light complexion, he was referred to by many of the white police officers in the precinct as the "white nigger." My father, on the other hand, "would not let them embarrass him. He looked them in the eye, said what was on his mind, responding in-kind, but professionally." Wallace also recalled comments by white police officers indicating that if you killed a black policeman, it was okay: "nothing will happen to you." On the other hand, when blacks arrested whites, "they had to be very positive" about the situation.

After the black officers were moved to the main police headquarters located on Oglethorpe Street, they were not permitted to enter from the main entrance, the front of the building. They had to enter from the Habersham Street entrance, which was in the rear of the headquarters building. This area had its own lockers and activity room completely separate from the white officers' quarters, although a part of the same facility. Addtionally, during their initial weeks at the main headquarters of employment, the black officers were not allowed to use restrooms in the building. Lt.

John A. White recalled, "We were treated like animals. In order to use restrooms, we had to leave the precinct and go down the street to an area that was infested with folks who sold moonshine and use their restroom in order to relieve ourselves." The black officers were also faced with using the "colored-only" water fountains. James Nealy said, in a documentary, "White officers had card tables, a pool table and other things that they could use, but we couldn't go in the barracks."

Jim Crow Drinking Fountains at Police Headquarters

Retired Lt. White shared that the salary of black police officers was quite depressed relative to the steps allowed for other officers. After eleven years on the force, he was promoted to sergeant, which put him three steps below the

Police Chief Truman Ward 1948-1949

position of a new white recruit who was making three steps more than where Lt. White had started. This even caused dismay among the many white officers. Additionally, White commented on the use of shop files in which other police officers or superiors could place anything in a policeman's file without his knowledge. In some instances this resulted in several officers being fired for "the good of the service" without knowing why they were dismissed.

The original black officers neither arrested white people nor patrolled any main streets or white neighborhoods. They patrolled only black neighborhoods—primarily West Broad Street between Bay and Gwinnett Streets. They patrolled on foot; first alone then in pairs. At first, they were not assigned to patrol cars. They could not achieve a rank. They were forced to wear a different uniform than their white counterparts, and they could not wear it to or from work. When black officers entered the barracks on Habersham Street, they were greeted by posted signs that said they could not drink from the water fountains or use the restrooms.

In spite of the limitations, prejudice and disadvantages, they persevered. Former Police Chief Truman Ward was considered by Lt. John A. White as a teacher and mentor for the initial black officers. Ward was quoted, "I told them to use their heads, and they did. They were the right type of men to know what was going on. They knew we had to do things gradually because it was very unusual in the South to have black police officers."

Perhaps the biggest disappointment for any of the original black police officers was the health and retirement benefits, which they didn't receive until years later. Many of the Original Nine had to choose an option, which left their widows without funds after death in order to make it on the retirement pensions. The city of Savannah has been called on numerous times to aid the widows of the deceased Original Nine to help compensate for the inequities of retirement benefits for those who served in the mid forties and early fifties.

Major Willie Williams, a thirty-five-year veteran of the police department, wrote that as a newcomer to the police department in the late fifties, he had met most of the original black police officers and they taught him all he knew about police work. While much of the instruction was not academic and classroom style, it was responsible for his survival on the force. These men "were like brothers to me." He went on to say those officers were unique in their experience, knowledge, and overall know-how.

Most of the original black officers were paired in twos and walked beats. They were given five minutes to walk one block, which was strictly enforced by their white sergeants. In walking West Broad Street, now Martin Luther King, Jr. Boulevard, from Liberty Street and Union Station, black police officers were not to pursue suspects or felons who were on the other side of the street toward Montgomery Street and the historic places where whites lived.

Lt. John White recalled a situation in the late 1940s when he witnessed an accident in which a white driver ran into an automobile driven by a black person. In accordance with rules and the exact location and side of the street of the accident, he had to call for a superior white officer before writing a ticket to the white driver, who was clearly in the wrong. Sidney Barns was the senior officer on the scene and insisted that the ticket be written. The white driver commented that if John White, as a police officer, could not arrest him, he shouldn't be in a police uniform in the first place. The incident drew much attention, particularly as it proceeded to a courtroom setting where John White was required to testify.

James Nealy, Daddy's first patrolling partner, reported an incident at Morrison's Cafeteria where blacks attempting to enter were refused admittance by the management, who called white police officers patrolling the area. Eventually the city police department dispatched black officers to deal with the situation to avoid charges of harassment and police brutality. Lt. White also recalled that in the early days knives became more popular than guns. It was not uncommon on the weekend to see streaks of blood throughout the district from fights the night before. Black officers would make a point of looking for those carrying guns. They destroyed the knives instead of arresting people—an approach that advanced their greater acceptance in the community, preventing crime, rather than penalizing blacks disproportionately for the crimes committed.

Officer James Nealy in Uniform

In the words of former Savannah councilman David Jones, "The Original Nine took the bumps and grinds and stuck it out to make it easier for police officers like me who came along later. It was still tough when I came on the force, but when things got a little rough there were people like Sgt. White out there who said *take it easy, give it a chance.* The young officers around here today would not likely have made it past the first month in those days."

Perhaps Willie Williams, a long-time veteran of the Savannah police department, summed it up appropriately: "It's not a survival of the fittest. It's the wise, not the strong who survive."

But we kids didn't know anything about that. Daddy was bigger than life to us. He was a policeman. He was a powerful kind of guy, authoritative. He was a combination of disciplinarian and the one who set the standards, even though Mama had a way of winning out when she wanted to. I had a great deal of respect for him and also didn't want to be at odds with him. I also knew he had a tough side that would set me straight. I felt a combination of wanting to please him and be respectful, knowing he was a big deal as a policeman in Savannah. And he did feel well-respected. I think he had no idea that the fellows he knew who were selling insurance, etc. were doing a whole lot better than he was financially. But Daddy enjoyed the fact that he was a celebrity in many respects. And our family felt special, too, because Daddy was a policeman.

CHAPTER 6
LAURA MAE

The role of wife and mother of four children in an average family took on new meaning when it became a policeman's family in the late 1940s. While all families struggled to make ends meet, in a policeman's family it took working together to fully nourish, encourage, protect, develop, teach values, and provide the ultimate support for launching children into adulthood. Job pressures from work came home and created monumental stress over and above what other families may have experienced.

What type of woman, wife, and mother could handle that? A storybook topic in her own right, Laura Mae was a woman who stuck through it all, sacrificed a professional career in nursing, and developed unique communication and people skills. She was respected by doctors, lawyers, teachers, hourly wagers, gainfully employed, underemployed and

William J. and Laura M. Day's Wedding Picture

the unemployed alike. Therefore, this book is also a story
about a wife and a mother, not the "woman behind the
man," but the "woman with the man" through thick and
thin. Officer William E. Wallace described Laura Mae as
being protective of William, or James, as she called him,
from unnecessary intrusions. Using Daddy's middle name
seemed to be her way of establishing her relationship with
him because no one else called him James.

My parents were married in April, 1938, and William Day Jr., my brother, came along in 1942. I followed two years later, and Edmund, our disabled brother, arrived in 1946. The youngest, Robert, was born in 1955. On a household income of $170 per month, with an invalid child, (quadriplegic and unable to speak) and a total family of six to feed, it was not easy in the late '40s to make ends meet. Many families have one or several major challenges in life that test individuals and the whole group. Frankly, having one member of the family with a steady job with regular income was a true blessing. On the other hand, having a child who was injured at birth drew on the family's strength, patience, and compassion. Mama at one time worked toward a Practical Nursing Diploma at Flowers Nursing Home on 36th Street between Florance and Burroughs. I'm sure she was glad for this training when Edmund came along.

Strong, yet loving and gentle, Laura Mae was well suited to be the mother of boys. We all had different personalities. William, the first-born, was always in the "in" crowd. He sang with a calypso group, was an athlete, joined a college fraternity, and majored in Math. I was blessed with above average academic ability and I involved myself with many activities, ranging from sports to student government, including student body president. I was generally a straight arrow, but I could be daring if the reward was worth it. Robert has been more like Daddy in his demeanor, his job

Laura Mae Day's Graduation

frustrations, and his life. A private person, he keeps his feelings to himself and doesn't talk them out. As a post office supervisor, he feels he hasn't gotten further along because he speaks his mind. We are all college graduates and I believe we were raised to be leaders—thanks in no small part to Laura Mae.

Mama was also a great cook. Laura Mae's kitchen was well known to the neighborhood and tenants in the two-story apartment building we owned. We were never latchkey kids coming into a dark or empty home. The aroma of food as we reached the front porch always welcomed us back. There was never a friend or relative stopping by who wouldn't be invited to have some collard greens and neck bones, boiled potatoes, beans, field peas, grits, fried fish or chicken. Her okra and greens were always seasoned with hamhocks, oxtail, or something like pig feet to give them a special taste.

But you would seldom find chitterlings cooking in our kitchen. Daddy hated the stink of chitterlings. They took a long time to clean before cooking, and they would shrink in volume when cooked. Strangely enough, it was only later in life that I realized they weren't good for you either. Attention to health in those days did not include examining products for their contents or for calories, carbohydrates, and saturated fats. Thank God, for we never would have tasted such great soul food.

Laura Mae's cooking was unmatched, and she was known to have the best fruitcakes ever baked, including the world renowned Claxton Fruitcake. W.W. Law, who was president of the local NAACP chapter, was also a local postman for the U.S. Postal Service and mail carrier on our block. He had personal experience with Laura Mae's fruitcake, as did the trash removers, friends, relatives and

---

Laura Mae's Fruit Cake Recipe

½ lb. butter	1 lb. white seedless raisins
1 cups granulated sugar	1 lb. candied cherries
4 eggs	1 lb. candied pineapple
2 cups All-purpose Flour	1 small bottle (1 oz.) lemon flavor
1 tsp. baking powder	1 small bottle (1 oz.) vanilla flavor
	5 cups of pecan halves

- Preheat oven to 250 degrees F. Grease (2) 9 x 5 inch loaf pans. Line the pans with brown paper*, which has been cut to fit, and then grease the paper.
- Sift flour and baking powder.
- Fold the candied fruit and pecans into the flour mixture.
- Cream butter and sugar.
- Add eggs – do not separate.
- Gradually add flour, fruit and pecan mixture and flavorings to the creamed mixture until all has been added.
- Add the flour and gently fold into the fruit and nut mixture.
- Pour batter into pans and bake in preheated oven for 2 ½ hours or until toothpick comes out clean.
- Cool in pan 10 minutes then remove from pan to wire rack(s) to cool completely.
- Cakes should be wrapped first in wax paper and then in aluminum foil and placed in airtight container. For storage, place in refrigerator or wrap for freezing. Cakes will keep indefinitely**.

*With the types of pans on the market today, it is not necessary to line with brown paper, but the pans need to be greased and floured. However, if preferred, parchment or wax paper can be used for lining. (Unlike the brown paper, they do not need to be greased after placing in the pan.)

Note: While Mama did not list in the recipe, she soaked the cakes with a dark rum or bourbon and wrapped tightly in wax paper and aluminum foil to hold the moisture. She repeated the soaking occasionally.

**After pouring the alcohol of choice over the cake, wrap with cheesecloth plus wax paper or plastic wrap and then with aluminum foil before placing in an airtight container. This will help the fruit cake retain its moisture and good taste.

others, because that was a standard holiday gift.

Baking started three to four weeks before Christmas. I can still remember the nuts of all types, the candied fruits, the batter, and the brown paper used to line the heavy, generously greased pans. It was an event as notable as the holiday itself that turned out at least two dozen cakes every year. In an interview before his death, W.W. Law still remembered how great Laura Mae's cakes tasted.

Laura also baked terrific chocolate cakes and sweet potato pies. There was nothing so splendid as the rich texture of real whipped potatoes that were creamy, enfolded by a deep-dish crust and rising above the pan. Her sweet potato pies were so magnificent, they inspired me and my wife Joy, to write one genuinely serious poem on Mama's birthday in 1970.

Our family became members of St. Matthew's Episcopal Church on West Broad and Anderson Streets. We attended with the Blounts, the McMillans, the McDews, the Wilsons, the Fords, the Hunters, the Jamersons, the Pattersons, the Gadsdens, the McCounts, the Laws, the Sullivans, the Winns, the Byers, the Wallaces, the Greens, the Flemings, the Glovers, the Haggins, the Rossers and a host of other families that watched our behavior as kids in the neighborhood, church, and anywhere else. And of course, there was the Rector, Father Caution, and his family.

Laura Mae was also a matchmaker of many relationships,

To Mama

Here is every wish for your
              enjoyment on today,
And may it bring happiness
              always your way.
May you get younger in spirit
              as the years go by,
For we have all enjoyed your enthusiasm
              even in baking potato pie.
You have worked hard over the years
              in raising all boys in a home.
The task was great, Mama,
              as you and Daddy stood it all alone.
So many thanks for your goals you did win
From one son and family
              on whom you can always depend.

CHARLES AND JOY
APRIL 1970

Sweet Potato Pie Poem

46

a counselor for those who were in deep financial or medical situations, and a finder of children from within the bigger family for those friends who were in need of a child. She helped with the adoption of a daughter for my godparents, the Ross's, and for Daddy's best friends, the Olivers, a son. Before formal adoptions became acceptable and easier for families, her efforts were deeply appreciated as heartfelt and moving expressions of love. Laura Mae cared deeply about families, her own, and for the Shaws in Hinesville– her family of origin.

Mama was the youngest of thirteen kids. Her brothers and sisters had complexions that ranged from one extreme of the spectrum to the other. While she was olive brown, the complexion one of my favorite aunts, Janie Porter, was extremely dark . On the other hand, Alma Watts, the aunt who lived closest to us on West Broad Street, and her family were all of medium-brown complexion. I must say I wondered about this as a kid. I came to the conclusion that our family heritage had been mixed generations ago, and because Mama was younger, she got to stay indoors in the kitchen and all of this contributed to her being light in complexion. Our town–like most perhaps–was, however, even within the black community, "skin-color sensitive." How unfortunate. Here we had a family of sisters from one end of the color spectrum to the other, and in their very community some would judge one over the other as having it easier, being more attractive, or more in or out of touch with the black masses.

It was through my Mama's side of the family that I was exposed to farming, ate the best buttermilk biscuits ever made, saw wringing of a chicken's neck, and shortly afterwards had the freshest (almost too fresh!) fried chicken on the table for dinner. Relatives either owned small farms or parcels and others were sharecroppers in Hinesville and Glenville, Georgia. They grew corn, greens, okra, peas, butter beans, sugar cane, tobacco, watermelon, potatoes, squash, and cotton. We took regular day trips during harvest season for fresh vegetables with my Uncles John and Lonnie Shaw, Mama's brothers.

Aunt Janie and Uncle Roland (Porter) were sharecroppers. They really had a "back forty" farming area to grow food for themselves. They were given a house with free rent and a small monthly stipend, but never owned anything. When Uncle Roland died of cancer, Aunt Janie had to give up the house and farm to another sharecropper family and move into a trailer parked in Hinesville near her other sisters and family farm. How traumatic this must have been for her.

In the city, with other relatives, we watched the Daddy Grace (of the International House of Prayer) parades on the porch of Uncle Howard and Aunt Alma (Watts). They lived on West Broad Street (now Martin Luther King, Jr.

Boulevard) north of Council's Lounge and the YMCA at Gwinnett. They were almost directly across from St. Phillips AME Church.

Mama was constantly busy, but she always had the time for encouragement for her kids and those she was around. It's amazing what memories stick with kids over the years. I recall my first crack at cooking breakfast, which was scrambled eggs, made with milk as I had watched Mama do, and wieners that were sliced open so that there appeared to be twice as many. I fixed toast too, but even that wasn't a cinch because I had to watch it in the oven with the broiler on and remember to turn it half way through the cycle. Mama raved over that breakfast as if it were the most gourmet meal that she had ever tasted and she even had tenants come in to take a sampling. At over sixty years of age that still feels good to me today.

Mama also acknowledged our abilities to do home and building repairs and to perform well at athletics. Once, while visiting in Hinesville, I did a scissors crossing over a four-foot fence to unlatch a gate. Mama expressed admiring amazement and astonishment that I had such a gift and ability to jump from a standing position and clear the fence without trouble. That too, made me feel good. The down side was that my foot-long sneakers were buried in soft mud, which was not a good feeling for the rest of the stay.

Mama never had to come to school because we were in trouble, and she was there at home when we were working late on homework projects, making sure there were supplies, dictionaries, and the much consolidated encyclopedia set—not the full expensive one, but the smaller, relatively inexpensive, yet effective set. She intensely read papers, grades, and school outcomes with a level of concentration that made it clear that she cared.

She was not one to gloat about the success of her family or kids. Even if they had been available back then, she never would have ridden around with a bumper sticker to acknowledge her kids were honor roll students. Her style was to wait for special friends to be there and within our hearing proudly announce that we received an A on a term paper, had all A's on a report card or turned in a B+ on something that was really tough. This was her style of encouragement that always felt good. My nephew, William J. Day, III saw one of my better report cards she'd saved from early school that had only positive comments and all A's. He asked, "How'd you do this?" I explained it was easy knowing someone cared.

Athletics was important to our family because it connected us not only with the more academic students but with other teammates who were driven by competition, physical fitness and to some extent stardom and receiving a different kind of respect and recognition while in school.

We somehow received a rite of passage by being involved in sports. Occasionally we met up with conflict, the result of being on opposing teams or dating someone from a school other than where we attended.

Basketball and track were the approved sports in our family. Because of my invalid brother, football was not felt to be an option for the rest of the Day boys. After having good basketball experience and showing some talent, I received an invitation from Coach Frank Simmons at Beach High School to try out for football. On a summer day when we were painting one of the attached units, I slipped off while my brothers covered for me. I liked football and when I made the team, I then had to persuade Mama and Daddy that I'd be careful, wear pads, and use my head. The important thing was to assure them I would not get hurt and become a burden on them. It took more than one conversation. Seeing my determination to play, they permitted it, even though they had refused to let my older brother play. That gave me another great feeling of accomplishment, support, and encouragement. The worst that ever happened was a sore knee from catching too many button hook passes and a sore back from not always getting into a fetal position quickly enough after being tackled.

In the 1960s, football players played both offense and defense. I played tight end. To my recollection, my mother never attended one of my high school football games and only one basketball game while in high school. I don't remember the team we played, but I do remember my score of 27 points—an all-time high for me and during one of my best games.

One of my most painful experiences occurred in that game as well. Coach Ellington, a young man at the time, saw fit to swat me in the chest–a reprimand for inappropriate dunking. I had gotten caught up in the cheering and encouragement from the crowd. As a good student, team captain, and all around respectful guy, that dunk and the subsequent response from the coach was an unusual occurrence. And memorable even now! The most fortunate aspect of this whole incident was that my mother didn't see the lick I took from Coach Ellington.

During the old days of no lottery games, something called Bolita was a very popular nickel and dime game that was illegal in Savannah. Lots of folks made a lot of money off of Bolita the same as the state and local lotteries do today. Although Bolita was illegal it didn't keep Mama, I believe, who had anose for games of chance, from sampling this game by having friends put a few pennies into the game on special occasions. One of those special occasions was when Uncle Shing (James Day) came from Ocala, Florida, to visit with us. He had a habit of drinking his coffee and turning his cup over into the saucer at the end so that he could read the grounds for a number that would likely hit that day. Telephone calls were in code; something like, "I need two cows twice with one bucket of milk as soon as you can and by Friday. Thank you." This meant the number 221 was thought to be the one to hit.

Some of the most fun times that I recall for Mama were when members of the St. Augustine Guild from St. Matthew's Episcopal Church and others that included educators and administrators in the neighborhood assembled on a Friday or Saturday at our house. People like Liz (Lula) Blount, Addie Byers, Virginia Wynn, Minnie Wallace, Essie Nealy, Alethia Priester, and Rosalyn Griffin would come to play a game called Pokeno. Occasionally there would be a game of Bid Whist. They also played Bonanza. These are board games that require plenty of pennies that are put in a circle with a combination of cards and bingo to determine winner and outcome. It appeared to me as a kid that these games would go on late into the night, as late as 10:00 p.m., which was late for working people, before a winner was declared with two or three dollars to take home. That was the level of reward for hundreds of dollars worth of excitement–or so it seemed to us hearing the laughter and happy voices coming from the living room.

The big reward for us, however, was finding plenty of goodies left on the card tables in the living room where peanuts, candies, and all kinds of treats waited. It was a pleasure to help Mama clean things up and then be rewarded with compliments for being such a good helper.

Other times I recall Mama really feeling happy include when, as an employee of a major airline, I took advantage of family trip passes and arranged three fun trips for her. The first was to Hawaii in the 1970s when we traveled together from Chicago to San Francisco and awaited a jumbo 747 airliner to the island of Oahu. Not knowing the ritual for waiting quietly until all full revenue passengers have boarded, Mama bellowed out mid-way in the boarding process, "Boy, we'd better get on this airplane before they leave us." I didn't have the nerve to tell her we had to see if space was left for us to even board, or else we would be looking for a hotel in San Francisco for the night and trying again the next day.

Well, God is good! We not only got on the flight, but we were seated in first class with all the china, tablecloths, and amenities. I also recall how Mama was getting so much service they kind of rushed her through the salad and bread for a second course. I looked over only to see my Mama, the quiet, gentle lady, wrapping a sourdough roll in a paper napkin and reaching for her purse. When she saw me looking, she exclaimed with that charming and affectionate look she had, "Well, it tastes too good to be thrown away; I'll eat it later." That was my Mama, unassuming, being herself anywhere in the world or sky.

Another trip with Mama was to Las Vegas, which ended up being Reno, because we couldn't get on the flight. I was all set to get her to see a heavyweight fight and lead her to the five-cent slot machines. We couldn't board to Vegas, and I thought "What the heck, let's go to Reno and see the fight on closed circuit." That turned out to be a great idea. I enjoyed some real quality time with my Mama. The highlight of this trip was Mama joining me at the blackjack table and putting down a two-dollar bet and then ordering a drink, which takes at least ten to fifteen minutes for the waitress to bring back – I believe by design. In four minutes, Mama ran out of money with her twenty-dollar bill and I would shove her a five or ten to keep her in the game–just to be there when the waitress showed up with the "free" drink. Finally, when the drink appeared, Mama scooted off the stool at the blackjack table, and I had run out of tens.

Inspired by this time with Mama, I wrote a speech on the self-reliance of blacks and other minorities on the way home on the plane. I talked about the value of doing things for yourself and moving on, as opposed to blaming others for how tough life may be. I got to present it at a conference of black professionals at my airline and it seemed to give me a higher profile among peers and upper management. Thank you, Mama, for that inspiration.

Finally, a more serious trip with Mama included one of her special friends, Rosalyn Griffin, who was dying of cancer which I did not know at the time. Mama called to ask me to include Ms. Griffin on the trip planned to Nassau, Bahamas, and without hesitation, I worked it out. My wife, Joy and I, my brother Robert (then in his early twenties), Mama, and Ms. Griffin were off for the Caribbean. Mama and Ms. Griffin really enjoyed their moments of togetherness as we catered to their every need. I felt good about being able to make arrangements. Ms. Griffin died within months after that trip!

When I think about my mother, who had all of the normal pressures of life with the added weight of being a policeman's wife and the worry that went along with that occupation, I always remember that she cared for a disabled child that required minute-by-minute attention twenty-four hours a day. I also think of the extended family of tenants, many of whom had their own serious troubles. I am really amazed at how she was so self-confident, had such impact and influence as a counselor, and always maintained her own peace of mind. Laura Mae was not just a wife of a policeman and a great mother; she was a loving partner in a committed relationship, devoted to family and friends.

We now have terms like "emotional intelligence" and "enlightened leadership." Mama embodied these skills long before there were names for them. A woman of ordinary education who was a genius in working with people, she had a gift for befriending the sometimes unfriendly. I had no idea of Mama's influence until years later. She gave us a genuine appreciation of how to be right with people at all levels in life.

CHAPTER 7
EDMUND

Edmund Moses Day's Infant Picture

Edmund was William and Laura Mae's third son. He was delivered by forceps, causing spinal injury which left him paralyzed, bedridden, and without the ability to speak for his whole life. The magnitude of this event was all encompassing. It affected who we were and how other families viewed us. The attention and extra work required altering careers, and all plans every day were centered on tending to a child needing continuous care, with diapers and hand feeding for twenty years to come.

When Edmund was born, at first it felt like I had a baby doll to play with. It was fun. Eventually, it got to be serious work and attention, especially as he grew. He would laugh, drool, and cry like a baby throughout his life, never growing into a man as his brothers were privileged to do. We all helped exercise his legs and muscles, and feed and attend to him. Mama changed most of his diapers, but we all pitched in at times. Everyone in the family was his caretaker. We felt his presence every minute of being home. If you were in the house, you knew how Edmund felt. Every one in the house knew how Edmund felt. He was never left alone mentally and hardly ever physically in a separate room. Everyone always knew how Edmund was doing.

Someone had to be home all the time to watch after him and respond to his cries. As a result, we almost never were able to go places as a whole family.

Edmund was very thin and tight and unable to speak. He only responded to hot, cold, pain, hunger, and being tickled. All he could do was a knee-jerk reaction, but we could understand what he meant. We grew up with him and played with him in his bed. We didn't bring people in a lot. Most people were afraid of Edmund's affliction, felt sorry for him, or thought he was a bad sight to look at. But this was our brother. Edmund was always in his room. We seldom took him on the porch or went places. When we did take him places, the fear and remarks of others made it all worse.

Ironically and in some strange way, Edmund's birth was a defining moment that brought family members closer and made us all caregivers. It must have affected Mama more than anyone would ever know, but she never showed it. Edmund was an extremely attractive boy with curly hair, heavy eyebrows and a well-proportioned face. His arms and legs were stiff and underdeveloped and required daily exercise flexing the muscles -- in which we all took turns. It was eight years before Mama had another child. I have wondered what thoughts were going through her mind while carrying and delivering her youngest.

The other special aspect of having an invalid child is that our house became the center for most activities involving the family. There were very few family trips, and many events the entire family could not attend. There were few family excursions; not because of family embarrassment, but because of travel difficulty and others being so disturbed by the sight of Edmund.

When Edmund would scream out for attention, it usually sounded as a threatening alarm and caused reaction with the ordinary passerby. Edmund loved to be tickled in the tummy and would give you that huge laugh that still tears me up today when I think of his innocent predicament and suffering. Yet Edmund would, like any infant, let you know when he was hungry, needed to be turned, or that something was uncomfortable about his bed.

The most painful time for our family was in the sixties, when we had to put Edmund into an institution when he was close to twenty. His older brothers had gone off to college, and his care had become too much for Mama. It was very traumatic for her, and when Mama became paralyzed from the neck down after an accidental fall in 1985, I wondered if she felt unjust treatment by God given the day-to-day care she had given an invalid child for so many years.

Edmund died in 1967 at the age of twenty. Bill and I had moved on and, in his way, Edmund did, too. I think I can speak for my whole family when I say we will never forget Edmund. The care we gave him as an infant made us all more caring people and also more sensitive to the handicapped or disabled. We love you, Edmund, and we miss you.

CHAPTER 8

FROM YAMACRAW VILLAGE

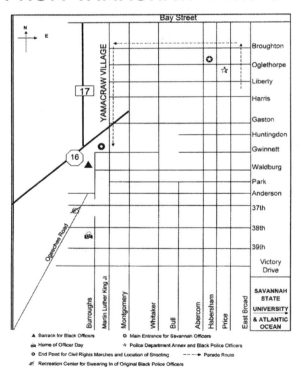

Yamacraw Village and Savannah City Map

The first few years of my life, our family lived in close quarters with other families in attached units subsidized by the government. This might have meant the "projects" in many folks' background. But Yamacraw Village was more highly respected by residents and the community alike. Families were fortunate to qualify for admittance. It meant that they had potential to do even better. This certainly was true for Daddy and Mama. The experience as a policeman, a Good Samaritan, and involved citizen in this environment made for some interesting stories.

Some 4,000 years earlier, the occupants were Archaic Indians, who are also credited with developing the first pottery in North America. Archaeologists also believe that small mammals, ice age mammoths and giant bison were early inhabitants from as far back as 12,000 years ago.

Savannah Waterfront and Eugene Talmadge Memorial Bridge

Recent history credits James Edward Oglethorpe as the founding father of Savannah. Oglethorpe glued together some thirty-five families who arrived on shore February 12,

1733, under the direction of King George II. Oglethorpe's mandate was to colonize Georgia and extend British ownership and trade. Oglethorpe, who became a general in 1765, found Creek and Cherokee Indians inhabiting Yamacraw Village near the Savannah River.

Oglethorpe made friends with Tomochichi, Chief of the Yamacraws, and received permission from them for settlement of the 13th colony. Tomochichi, his wife Senauki (also, Scenaukay) and nephew Toonahowi were later acknowledged for their generosity with a trip to England where they met the Archbishop of Canterbury, the English trustees and King George II along with Queen Caroline.

Oglethorpe and the early settlers credited Tomochichi for their survival. Tomochichi's burial site, dated 1737, can be found today in Savannah in Wright Square. Within 100 years, practically all Indians were gone from Savannah and Georgia. The Native Americans were either required to move west of the Mississippi River or were killed or died of common diseases.

It is ironic that Yamacraw Village, named in honor of the encampment by the Creek Indians with Tomochichi, would later become a government housing village inhabited by "up and coming" black families. Nestled near the Savannah River, the complex was within walking distance to downtown Broughton Street. The river, which demarcated Georgia and South Carolina, was draped with an exceedingly tall bridge named in honor of the late Eugene Talmadge, who campaigned in the state of Georgia on the white supremacy platform. The new Eugene Talmadge Memorial Bridge replaced an old structure in 1991 and increased the clearance on the Savannah River from 137 feet to 185 feet, opening the harbor to 98 percent of the world's shipping fleet.

In 1947 these subsidized housing units looked almost new. The project was developed in the early 1940s with some 480 units as part of an urban renewal effort by the city. At the city's entrance, some sixty blocks of frame houses, which had become an eyesore, were cleared. The city housing authority's applications for residence had strict requirements for employment and level of income to ensure that the complex was maintained above the normal run-of-the-mill government housing projects.

The neighborhood was kept clean and there were well-maintained recreational areas with playground equipment in different sections of the development. There were ice boxes, but no refrigerators in those days. We met some of our lifelong friends in Yamacraw Village. This is where William and Laura Day met Willie and Elizabeth Blount and who remained friends for life. Liz Blount recalls that, in the late 1940s, rent was based on income and ranged from approximately $30 to $38 per month.

By being a policeman's family, we were given special consideration and respect because everyone liked having a policeman in their block. There were many cases where Daddy's level-headedness in emergencies and crises paid off many times over for our family and the neighbors.

Even though I was very young, I can distinctly recall accidents occurring in the park only a few yards from our unit, which required a cool head and some knowledge of how to stop bleeding or checking for broken bones. I don't recall waiting for an ambulance to come in those days, but I do recall Daddy using two plain boards and tape to set a youngster's leg before driving him to the hospital.

Perhaps the most graphic experience involved a youngster who was wearing no shoes and riding a bike too big for him. This looked like a disaster waiting to happen and it did. One of the little boy's toes was severed in the spokes of the bike immediately resulting in a chaotic scene–blood all over the sidewalk, screaming neighbors, kids jumping up and down, and someone who thought to bang on our door for help. Fortunately Daddy was at home. I didn't realize policemen were trained as paramedics in those days, but I do remember him calming the scene, causing people to disburse, giving room for the youngster to breathe, putting on a bandage and stopping the bleeding. He had the foresight to also take the severed toe and race to the hospital. I'm not sure if that toe was saved, given surgical procedures available in those days, but the mere fact that someone would think of picking up a body part in a crisis situation was pretty impressive to me.

These little incidents didn't just happen to other people. In some instances one of us was directly involved. To lay the backdrop, it was wintertime and close to a holiday. On the prior weekend we had gone to visit relatives "in the country," at Hinesville, Georgia. The family returned with the usual goodies, including harvested vegetables, canned food, and a croaker sack filled with paper shell pecans. Paper shell pecans are easy to shell and delicious to eat. Back at home, I couldn't get enough of those pecans, and I knew they were stashed away in a downstairs closet. I'm not sure if I knew too much about flashlights at five years of age or didn't want to turn on the electrical switch to awaken my sleeping Mama and Daddy, but I chose a box of Diamond strike-on-the-box matches to help me see once I got into the closet. With about a third of the match burned down the wooden stem, I saw what I was looking for and accidentally dropped the match. I couldn't believe how fast a dry croaker sack could ignite and begin to burn! I do remember trying to close the door to smother everything, before deciding my best bet was to panic, yell as loud as I could, and figure out a way to pretend I didn't do anything wrong later on. Between my yelling and the smoke, Daddy once again came to the rescue, using a quart jar to throw water on the blaze. As he dashed back and forth, I stayed clear, amazed with his swiftness of movement and relieved that I didn't burn the whole place down. Mama became the detective, pulling me aside in the kitchen to get all of the pertinent facts without raising her voice. She told me to stay there and she'd be back. She went to brief Daddy while she was bandaging his burned hand, which was also cut when the glass jar had broken.

The next thing I heard was, "Charles, your daddy wants to see you upstairs"–words I dreaded more than most anything. Corporal punishment was not outlawed in Georgia, certainly not in Yamacraw Village, and I can absolutely assure you it wasn't in our home when I was growing up. That was the calmest and worst spanking I can ever recall as a kid, but somehow it made me feel better because the score was even. I didn't get the safety lesson until a day or two afterwards when all had calmed.

The final story of living in Yamacraw Village that I can recall happened during the summers, particularly in July and August, when there was sweltering heat. In the absence of a swimming pool in the park, the public works folks would turn on a sprinkler. There were a couple of older kids who seemed to be determined to make that small playground into a swimming pool. The practice was to pull the lid off of a large drainpipe and to dunk one's self or be dunked into the opening–a dangerous way to cool off. It wasn't possible to swim with the small opening, but there were ladder handles for the water sewer department employees to lower themselves. That was the only saving thing for one kid who couldn't get out on his own. Help arrived, once again including my father the policeman, to haul the near-drowned soul to safety. These events gave me a chance to see the role of a police officer on and off duty, up close and personal. They, in fact, seemed to be the heroes who were called on for any type of an emergency.

In 1949, the biggest move of my young life and certainly for Daddy and Mama as young adults was about to happen. We were leaving Yamacraw Village and some of our friends and moving to a totally different neighborhood on the west side of Savannah This was a major step because it was a self-contained house, gigantic in size, two stories, with high ceilings and consisting of four separate dwellings: 2204, 2206, 2208, and where we lived, 2210 Burroughs Street. Daddy and Mama would be the owners of their first home—an apartment building. I don't know exactly how he did it, but Daddy was a put-away kind of a guy and probably cut some deals. The point is, he did it. By my calculations, this property was bought for just under $7,000 with approximately $750 down payment. That left a balance of $6,250, which netted out over a 10- to 12-year payback, with payments of $62.50 per month. This must have been a bold move to double the cost of housing from the previous rent at Yamacraw Village. I remember the $62.50 quite well because in the late '40s and '50s writing checks wasn't very common–at least not in my neighborhood. More typically, my older brother Billy or I would run in to drop off cash payments in envelopes at the bank, utility and telephone company, or clothing store, while Daddy or Mama double-parked.

Day Family's Burroughs Street House

This "new" house would be the place where our family would live for the next twenty-three years until my father's death. The house faced west, had an alley on its side for trash collection, access to our backyard with a detached garage, and a small piece of turf in front on which to play. There were only two or three homes facing Burroughs Street in our block. The street originally was dirt and occasionally was scraped smooth by a construction tractor with a large blade under its belly. The process included filling in and resurfacing with a clay-like dirt and was an exciting sight to watch as a kid..

Our house and most houses in our neighborhood, were heated with kerosene. The kerosene was stored in large tanks inside backyards off the alley way. Our tank sat on an upright stand near the rear of the house. In addition to city and utility vehicles, the alley was used by an elderly man with nub fingers who drove a fuel truck that supplied us and our neighbors with kerosene. The old man was accompanied by his grandson who assisted his grandfather by pulling the fuel hose over fences and through yards to fill the tanks.

The youngster assisting his grandfather was Clarence Thomas, the United States Supreme Court Justice.

The move to the new Burroughs Street house was traumatic for many reasons. I was leaving everything that was familiar: all my friends, what I did every day, looked at, and saw. People in the South didn't really move a lot, much less far away. I was much too young to know that, though I felt it. Even though we stayed on the west side, a move across town was a big deal.

The change felt sudden, and the new home was a foreign looking place that seemed scary—even dangerous. First, it had its own back yard. The house seemed extremely large, with each room having a fireplace and chandeliers with gas lanterns for light. It wasn't long after we moved in that the gas fixtures were rewired for electricity and the fireplaces were sealed to use kerosene heaters and these were later changed to gas heaters for each room. There was no central air conditioning and heating system in those days.

I started kindergarten shortly after moving to Burroughs Street. Even though I didn't want to leave Mama, going to school and making new friends helped in the transition. School, friends and having my first girlfriend, sort of, were the only things that saved me.

One other thing was also fairly traumatic as a five-year-old moving into this house. The kitchen had a coal and wood stove that also served to heat the room. It was vented like a Benjamin Franklin fireplace and sat fairly low to the floor with cast iron covers and a hook to remove what would be heating plates on a regular stove. Our move must have been during cold weather because that heater was on. My inaugural event in the new house occurred when I sat on the heater to rest, not knowing I would end up with a gigantic mark to remind me of the event for life. I didn't know the song "Rise up All Men of God! Have Done with

Lesser Things," but that may have been a very appropriate tune given the circumstances.

For my folks—and Daddy in particular—to move on and make a risky investment, banking on renting out three-quarters of a building that we would always consider our home, was very gutsy. It had a flavor of entrepreneurial spirit that seemed to have caught on in our way of thinking. My siblings and I have run our own businesses, managed real estate properties, and used the skills of fix-up to take care of our own homes and families–all learned from watching and helping Daddy, the entrepreneur. Many people would never have been so bold.

The new setting with just a few houses in the same block allowed us to post basketball racks on one side of the street and to have plenty of space to play. Daddy arranged this by getting permission from an elderly family whose house faced 38th Street, leaving their backyard an open area with a fence for attaching a substantial rack. It was there that we all learned to play basketball and we played with half of the neighborhood. Eventually, my brothers and I each played on some team in every school we attended. Basketball also provided a source for "grant and aid," now known as scholarships, in order for us to complete studies at Savannah State University.

Our house became the neighborhood play center because of the distance of the nearest playground that blacks were permitted to use. A large group gathered weekdays after school and when homework was done. They also showed up on weekends. Well, this meant we, the kids in the family, had another opportunity for testing entrepreneurial enterprise. I got the bright idea, with Mama's help, to buy day-old doughnuts which came three in a package for a nickel. I would heat them up and cover them with chocolate topping made from confectioner's sugar and cocoa. Warming got the doughnuts over the "day-oldness" and the icing spread over them increased the value and attractiveness—especially given no competition. I sold them at a nickel a piece from a large tray. This was a big hit with the crowd that we drew.

There was no need to worry about cutting the lawn at this house. The sidewalk was only about four feet from the steps of the house, and a large sycamore tree was the only real sign of growth on the dirt street, which was eventually paved up to the sidewalk. We played marbles and horseshoes and putted golf balls with a driver in the "front yard" all in a space of about forty square feet, which in those days seemed like a quarter of a football field.

Perhaps the biggest thing that happened in that neighborhood during the civil rights activism was a deliberate plan to take over a park that was only a block away. At the corner of 37th and West Broad, now Martin Luther King Drive, a school used the park for recess. At that time the schools were still fairly segregated. Outside of school hours, white children who lived east of West Broad Street would use the park and anyone of color would be chased off, even sometimes by police. This all came to a head in the early '60s, when I was 18. The groups assembling on the west side of West Broad Street for regular basketball games started going as a team or group to play on the heretofore non-integrated park. A number of scuffles went on from time to time, but eventually the park was shared and we all got to play.

While this was a fairly traumatic occurrence for the neighborhood, it too passed and we all went on enjoying living within walking distance of a new-found playground. I could walk to elementary, junior high, and high school from our new home, and the bus stop was close, too. Plus, we were just around the corner from my uncle who had a TV. We could also walk to a bus stop to downtown, the Florance Street Elementary School, the Charity Hospital, Alfred E. Beach High School, St. Matthew's Episcopal and other churches. We had Miss Mary's corner store, a neighborhood grocery store, and Mrs. Style's one-of-kind snowballs made from shaved ice with multiple choices of liquid syrup poured on top and throughout–delicious and cooling! Wow, was that worth moving from Yamacraw Village or what!

CHAPTER 9
FESS

No description of my father's life would be complete without mentioning his best friend Fess. Once or twice in a lifetime, we acquire a special pal and buddy unlike any other friend. There is trust, caring, and mutual support expressed and sometimes, oddly, verbal sparring that creates this kind of relationship. It can be a powerful bond on a special level with love much like the biblical relationship of David and Jonathan. Onlookers may interpret many exchanges as argumentative, but, in fact, what is occurring is a contest of wit, endurance, stubbornness, logic, and finally acceptance of being right or wrong.

Daddy had two such friends. The first was James Nealy, his partner on the police force where they came to trust each other with their lives. The second, and perhaps most memorable to me, was the Rev. Harry H. Oliver, who was pastor of several small churches in Savannah and nearby areas. Rev. Oliver, called Fess, was a fishing pal, checker player and fix-up man, and he was always Johnny-on-the-spot with our family.

The Reverend Harry Oliver

It sometimes looked like Rev. Oliver had a part-time job at our house. He was there quite frequently, particularly with projects like reconstructing the back stairs or some difficult type of plumbing problem that my brothers and I hadn't yet learned to fix. We were able to paint, change plumbing valves, unstop commodes, repair window panes, replace the pop rope pulleys in the frame of windows, remove and replace light fixtures, stop leaks in the sink, and remove the sink drain to free up a clog. But it was Rev. Oliver who was there when we stripped the wallpaper with a compressor, discovering small strips of wood and a filament material inside which we had to plaster over to form a smooth wall. This was before wallboard and I often wonder if that filament was packed with asbestos.

Daddy's best friend, Fess, was trusted more than any man that I've ever known to be friends with Daddy. He was trusted with Daddy's life, his wife, and his family. It would not be unusual to come home to see Rev. Oliver finishing up a project after Daddy had left for a shift or before he got home. Neither would it be uncommon to see Rev. Oliver helping Mama cut a few of her tough toenails and calluses. Fess helped us kids in many ways. When Daddy worked shifts where he was sleeping or was not at home when we were up and about, it was Fess who gave us a hand in fixing toys, getting a ride somewhere, or even sitting through a round of checkers. Fess was one of the few people who visited our house and sought out our invalid brother Edmund to spend time playing with him a bit and stretching his limbs–as we all did. Fess had no reluctance in helping out, including picking Edmund up and feeding him.

The real story about Rev. Oliver and my father is that they always argued. They both called each other Fess, presumably short for professor, to give credit and due that each knew something about most things that would enable him to argue more extensively. The nickname Fess came second to the nickname Chief in those days as a polite term to draw one's attention respectfully, especially in situations where you were meeting someone for the first time and really didn't remember, or know, the name. Daddy and Rev. Oliver were both fairly stubborn and set in their own ways, but couldn't get enough of working with each other on the simplest and more difficult projects—at least around our house and, on occasion, at Rev. Oliver's house across town in West Savannah.

Fess was an amazingly hard worker. He held a job at Savannah Cyanamid Mill and several other local plants. Rev. Oliver also preached at more than one church in rural areas surrounding Savannah. In addition, he was an insurance man who sold term insurance for a few pennies a week as a representative of the Pilgrim Insurance Company.

These $100, $200, and $500 insurance policies were very popular in Savannah's black community. Five-hundred-dollar policies meant a lot to families in my neighborhood, and if you had one you were considered "taking care of business." It was barely enough, in reality, to cover funeral expenses and headstones.

Fess competed for his business in our neighborhood with an older white man who carried a very thick rectangular book with seemingly a thousand pages on his door-to-door collection rounds. Daddy, I believe, helped Rev. Oliver understand the accounting process for keeping his books straight, reading the terms of the policies, and selling insurance to prospects. I'm also pretty sure Daddy and other close friends identified new clients for Rev. Oliver to keep things going.

It amazes me how Fess spent as much time as he did at our house and still took care of an entire family of his own. Mattie Oliver was Harry's wife for some fifty years. She was from South Carolina and had a true, delightful, Geechee accent that was easily distinguished among others with a natural southern drawl. She was one to stay home a lot and cherished her wood-burning stove. When we visited her home, it seemed as if something was cooking on the fire at all times. Mattie always referred to Fess as Rev. Oliver, and she was deeply religious. I believe she gave him a hand in preparing some of those down-home sermons he delivered in the rural churches, which had congregations of only twenty-five to thirty families. For a southerner, Mattie's speech was so fast that I would often have to ask her to repeat what she said, or alternatively, just say "Yes Ma'am."

In the old days, parents did spank their children in the name of discipline. Daddy had a razor strap he used on us. Fess used to whip his son Ralph. One time this upset their two German Shepherds so much that they attacked Fess. Ralph ran away from home, never to return. Years later, I heard he had joined the Navy. After some time had passed, my Mama sought to help them by putting out an "in-family search" for a newborn child that Mattie and Fess could adopt. Eventually, a child was found for Mattie and Fess and an exchange agreement was made between the birth mother and the Olivers. The term adoption wasn't used to explain the transfer of such a child within a family directly from the house where he or she was born. I am still puzzled about how people got proper birth certificates from midwives' deliveries.

This assistance by my family, and specifically my mother, filled an important void in the Olivers' lives. The results produced a robust, energetic, loved and well-cared-for son who went on to become a Navy Seaman and now has a family of his own with five children. We are still in touch with this son and his family as they provided information and pictures to assist with the development of this book.

The most heated argument between Fess and Fess (as they called each other) occurred in our back yard one summer. The two men were replacing–for the umpteenth time–some wooden stairs that rotted regularly because water spilled from the high roof where the gutters could not maintain the overflow during heavy rains. It is an art to cut a piece of wood at a right angle that is straight and fits perfectly on the left and right and across the center piece to build eight stairs that lay flat without wobble. Fess didn't like to use a tape measure as much as Daddy. In fact, he preferred "eyeing it." This always irritated Daddy because he didn't want to waste wood. Daddy marked his boards and was very precise with his cuts. He knew that eyeing it worked sometimes but would often cause a perfect right angle to be missed. This resulted in a longer job, and the wrong cut cost money and aggravation. Fess was usually very good at eyeing the cut, but Daddy insisted on using a square, since he had invested in all the appropriate tools for the job. Daddy worked on one board his way and Fess used his approach on the second board for the other side of the steps' frame. Fess went ahead eyeing the measurements on his side, using a fall-out of the previous cut as a guide that he would replicate for each slot in the wood.

Relationships with best friends can be fairly competitive, and the relationship with Fess and Fess was no exception. In this case, the Rev. Oliver finished many minutes before Daddy. Fess felt proud of his accomplishment. The problem came later at the time of fitting a board crossways. I could tell, as a little nail-carrying and hammer-fetching kid, that there was trouble brewing in that there yard. I never heard such terse language without cursing. I didn't know they could both speak so loudly. They were very close to each other, but it was also clear that this was not a fight; this was a war of words. I knew it was over when one of them stopped talking and the other got deathly quiet. Those two things are different. The one who stopped talking was really trying to let it go. The one who got quiet was still thinking about it and stewing. By the time the whole mess was straightened out, it was dark and we were using lights to finish the job. There was some strange thing about the relationship of these two men; they always got it done in spite of themselves.

That night, I think the make-up came when Rev. Oliver said at the end of the evening, "You were right!" and "Well, just to make you feel better, I'm going to take these scrap boards home for firewood to get them off of your hands." While the gesture was intended to be supportive, I could see the expression on Daddy's face–"You've got to be kidding! You're going to burn this expensive wood in your fireplace?" But all of a sudden they both started laughing like you never heard before. Boy was I relieved! I started laughing too, not sure why–guess I was just glad to see the steps done and that they were back to having fun!

As I said before, they both were stubborn, but at least Rev. Oliver was consistent with his stubbornness. He dug in his heels, whether in the back yard helping my father construct new stairs or sharing a meal with us in our yellow kitchen at the yellow table. (We had actually painted the table and the walls at the same time.) In the open wall cabinets, one of which was filled with canned and bottled food, Mama stored her hot green peppers in vinegar – the source of another great Fess tale. Fess always wanted the green pepper vinegar on his greens when he ate with us. He seemed to want to demonstrate his capacity to handle spicy foods. Putting the pepper with vinegar on greens was a great way to test this awesome ability!

One day Mama saved a hot jalapeno pepper that she had gotten from Hinesville. Rumor had it that this pepper would be capable of launching a man to the moon before anyone knew it was possible. At this particular sitting, I didn't know what was in store, but Mama was very, very cordial asking Harry if he would like some more collard greens, if he'd like to put some pepper on them, and if he'd like the pepper vinegar now.

He said "Yes, yes thank you. Yes, thank you, Ma'am". She proceeded to bring this special pepper out and politely said, "Harry, you should be careful with this pepper, it's very hot and a little different from some you might have had before." Harry took that as a challenge. He decided he'd have a mouthful of greens and bite down on almost half of that luscious green jalapeno pepper. It took about two or three seconds for the juices of that pepper to be felt.

When trouble started, I thought Rev. Oliver was choking because he had swallowed a whole piece of the oxtail or fatback used to season the greens. Being dark complexioned, it was quite a sight to see him turn red. He was the color of a beet and about to blow his greens across the room, but blocked the expulsion with his hands. He lost his voice, drank a quart of water, and was sweating from ear to ear. The funniest part of the episode was to see how caring Mama was after she had done this to Fess. She wanted to know if he was going to be okay, if she could get him more water, more greens on top of what he had. I have to give it to Rev. Oliver– he finished his meal, tearing and sweating, and without a voice. He mumbled something toward the end, thanking Mama before jumping in his car and speeding home.

Ultimately, the Reverend Harry Oliver became an assistant pastor at Stout Chapel on Richards Street in Savannah. He also served at St. Paul's CME Church on Barnard Street and was a "Son of the Church." I think that meant he was a minister in training, serving smaller churches. In total he worked with five churches, some of which were in the surrounding areas of Savannah, such as Irvington, Gordon and Richmond Hills. Continuing his insurance business, Rev. Oliver worked for Guaranteed Life Insurance Co., headed by Boyles Ford. In 1969, the company became Afro-American Insurance Co. and, Rev. Oliver cashed out of the firm and went back to being a carpenter and all-around fix-up man.

Daddy and Fess were truly devoted friends through most of their adult lives. They accepted each other, believed in one another, always offered support, valued each other, forgave mistakes, and just dropped by or called to say hi. They explained things that didn't make sense and, of course, yelled when the other didn't listen, which I feel was the sparring that kept them close and challenged to be the best friends they could be.

Though in many ways an average guy, Fess was a rock of a friend. He demonstrated that there were people in this world who worked hard, were trustworthy, and there for life. He still looms large in my mind.

CHAPTER 10
THE TENANTS

My father had managed not only to earn a college degree—a remarkable accomplishment—but he and my mother found a way to purchase some apartments. In addition to getting kids off to school, nursing Edmund, and tending to domestic chores, Mama was the office manager of tenant affairs for the rooms and apartments rented out at 2204, 2206 and 2208 Burroughs Street. All were connected to our two-bedroom unit at 2210.

A typical day included four or five tenants knocking on the door or ringing the bell in the center of the door to have a brief discussion with someone who was paying $5, $8, $10 or $12 for a room for that week. It was not uncommon for folks to fall behind, but we seldom, with a police officer landlord, had to worry about evictions. Instead, Mama, with a warm smile and personality, talked in a motherly fashion to tenants who often were twice her size. Some preferred buying alcohol over paying their rent. They all called her Mrs. Day and, with very few exceptions, delivered as promised, accepting her counseling about getting their lives together to move on, keeping a good job, watching their manners and not cursing, dressing correctly and not making noise in the house to bother the kids.

Some tenants even managed to work bartering deals such as helping with our laundry, which one of our most favorite tenants, Louise, did for years. But in reality, from Louise's frequency of presence in our kitchen when I came home from school, I think she made it up in food consumption.

Sgt. John White remembers that in the early days when black policemen started on the force, they would be in the street with people that they generally all knew. It would not be uncommon for them to have to arrest someone who was in a drunken rage or sleeping off a drunken stupor in a public place, and the next day be in a situation of socializing with them. Daddy was an exception to this rule.

Laura Mae, on the other hand, was accepting and would feed a tenant who seemed undernourished to her or practically anyone else who showed up at the door. There were some raucous times with renting rooms to men and women with girlfriends and boyfriends who got into fights. There was never a problem that Laura Mae couldn't handle directly, or if not, she'd place a quick call for a squad car to show up. It was even worse to get Daddy involved, who would probably be more inclined to book them than to do the psychological reasoning that Mama had developed with the tenants, whom she regarded as family.

Our tenants were many and varied. For instance, Louise worked at a laundry and often times did our laundry. I thought she was our maid. Marietta Baker, was a nurse—proper, thin and tall. Eunice, a very attractive woman, worked at Texas Instruments as a technician.

And then there were the week-to-week guys. Mama would always tell them, "When you get your checks, don't you make any stops before you come pay your rent." "Yes, Mrs. Day," they would answer. And they usually did.

When I was about twelve we had a tenant called Party Artie, whose style was debonair. One day we received the sad news that Party Artie had been out on the town and was shot dead in a simple argument, possibly over a woman. We'd grown to like the guy, and all the tenants were like extended family, so it was a loss for everyone. Removing Party Artie's belongings and not seeing him float in and out was fairly traumatic for all of us. All he left were some clothes, and that was the only payment we could get. Even though the clothes were great, Daddy didn't want any of us to ever wear any of them. I especially had my eye on a three-quarter length hound's-tooth jacket, so I was doubly disappointed.

On one other occasion, a Hunter AFB enlisted man entered our lives as a tenant at 2204. Lawrence played checkers with us for peanut butter and Ritz crackers and was also a very vibrant and youthful person. He became ill with a severe stomachache and was admitted to the Air Force hospital on base for what should have been ordinary surgery to remove his appendix. Lawrence died after the appendix ruptured during the surgery. This hit my brothers and me hard because he'd been like an older brother and was healthy and playing with us only two days earlier.

An unusual and fascinating quality of Laura Mae's was her acceptance of others in circumstances of family life that were controversial. A special tenant named Patsy moved into 2204 and stayed for over a year while transitioning into married life. During this time, I discovered she was our half sister from a relationship Daddy had before he married our mother. With arms wide open and a caring attitude, Mama made certain that unit 2204 was in top-notch shape and newly painted for Patsy. This demonstrated to me a unique quality given the situation she found herself in with a child of my father's, but not her own.

The apartments were constant work. Daddy spent a lot of time making us look on while he made repairs. We assisted him or he would let us do the job and he would oversee it. As we got older, we became the apartments' maintenance crew. Even though at the time I resented being "free labor," working instead of playing basketball or football, I benefited greatly from that experience. And, occasionally, my brother Bill did cover for me while I slipped out to practice. We learned painting, carpentry, plumbing, electrical, and gas system skills. As an adult, I felt confident enough to even install a furnace in my Chicago home. I will never forget those apartments and the many characters who inhabited them.

CHAPTER 11
MY FATHER, THE FISHERMAN

Saturdays off from work in the fifties, graced with reasonably good weather and no northeastern wind, meant going out for a daylong fishing trip with Daddy. Wilmington Island, some 8,000 acres in size, hosts a number of homes, yachts, country clubs, marinas, and launch pads for fishing boats. The parade of fishing boats in the early morning from Thunderbolt near the Thunderbolt Bridge and around Wilmington Island seaward was and is an awesome sight. This traffic is of great commercial importance in addition to being a pleasure for onlookers.

We would arrive at 6:00 a.m. at Solomon's on Wilmington Island and rent a small fishing boat or bateau (the Cajun French name for a lightweight flat-bottom wooden river boat used chiefly in Louisiana and Canada) that had room for up to four. Even without the boating conveniences of today–no cover, no head or portable potty, no steering wheel, no tape deck, music, radio, and definitely no cell phones—boy, what fun we had in anticipation of catching fish and crab with Daddy. We would all have cushions to sit on that doubled as life preservers, and when we were smaller we were required to actually wear an additional life jacket just in case. Our rods had floats on them for the inevitable incomplete cast and we also had a very well-equipped tackle box, a water cooler, and an ice chest with some favorite goodies. The most impressive treat was Daddy's famous cinnamon bun and sliced spiced ham laid across the top, which doubled for lunch or just a late-morning snack.

Happiness was being on the serene Wilmington River with freedom to move about to two or three great fishing spots including near the old DeSoto Hotel and somewhere near the Savannah Yacht and Country Club. When there was enough room on the boat, there was always a welcome guest. Of course the most popular guest was Rev. Harry Oliver, or Fess.

We had simple bait for starters, which included chicken necks for crabbing. Once in awhile we would throw in chicken backs to make it luscious for the creatures. Then there would be frozen shrimp, which would thaw for bottom fishing between the time we left home early in the morning and the time we needed them on the trip.

Daddy would be in charge of the ten or fifteen HP motor, which we brought with us to put on the rented bateau. Often the areas that we maneuvered through also required using oars. This enabled us to sneak up on those unsuspecting shrimp, minnows, and sometimes even mullet fish, too.

One of the more fascinating moments of the day was casting for live bait early in the morning using a shrimp net, which Rev. Oliver specialized in handling. Daddy would find the ideal creek, and Harry would be on the bow of the boat using the gap on the right side of his mouth where he was missing several teeth. This gap seemed designed for being able to grip one end of the net in his mouth and spread his arms with a rope from the center of the net tied to one of his wrists. The net with weights around its skirt would unfold with Rev. Oliver's cast looking like a lady's wide crinoline. Believe it or not, the net seemed to me, to be just that beautiful. I was always amazed that there was no bait in the process. No exchange, as with shrimp bait when fishing. Just a wide and quiet cast and a nudge on the rope, which pulled things to the center from the bottom of the net, bringing in all that was trapped as the net sank to the muddy bottom of the river or creek.

Pulling the net in was always exciting, awaited with curiosity and wonder to see what would come in. Old shoes and discarded cans would often be part of the lot. But more often than not there were at least several shrimp and occasionally fish, including those mullets. The next part was very messy–dumping out the net in the middle of the boat where everyone got wet and a little muddy, trying to hold our feet on the small bench across the bateau to avoid whatever debris spilled out along with the jumping shrimp. Harry Oliver seemed to have the toughest hands of all as he just picked up jumping shrimp, fins and all, and put them in a big well, which we carried submerged on the back of the boat. These live shrimp could have been purchased down the street from home at an exorbitant price. But this was a lot more fun in addition to being more cost effective, which I'm sure was on the minds of Daddy and Harry.

After the first hour or so of catching our own live shrimp, we were all set for an entire day of even more suspense and pleasure, a day on the water with Daddy. There were defined strategies in fishing cheaply as we did. We caught our live bait early in the morning, crabbed during the low tides, and then while tides were moving, we fished with the live bait in order to catch trout, bass, and more game fish. When the tide stilled, we then used dead bait to catch the old staples or bottom fish that we often loaded in our coolers–croakers, an occasional perch and even catfish. My favorite fish were the flounder and sheephead, both of which were tricky to catch since one lay flat on the bottom and the other would gently suck the bait. We would ease the line down to the bottom and, surprisingly, it would feel as if it were tied on the bottom, requiring help to reel it in. But what a feeling to see such a beautiful fish, so delicious that I could almost see it in Mama's pan and anticipate the taste.

I thought Daddy was the smartest fisherman on the waters. We oiled our reels, changed lines in between trips, and kept up with the latest spinners. Daddy studied the tides, knew the stages of the moon, and always checked weather reports for safety. He picked the best places to rent a boat and took great care in preparing for the day, keeping in mind how many kids and adults he wanted to include and the type of fishing appropriate for the season. It seems that once we reached our first fishing hole it took Daddy an inordinate amount of time to get ready. His first priority was always getting us, the sons, ready with a rod in hand and a baited line overboard into the water, ready for catching the first fish. That was a transitional moment for him. It almost seemed as if watching us fish was good enough for him to be satisfied with the trip. And it probably was.

Once in awhile we would have a guest fisherman, besides Daddy's best friend, Rev. Oliver. Some of the names I can't remember, but it seems the condition for going was that you had to be at least sixty years of age and didn't talk much. The one exception was Daddy's beat partner on the police force, James Nealy. I'm convinced Mr. Nealy was one of the luckiest men I ever knew, whether it was fishing or at the state fair playing bingo.

On other occasions we would take other senior citizens of Savannah who lived on our side of town. In one instance, I recall an older guest fisherman having a drop line, or a rope with a couple of hooks on it and a weight. He didn't have the nice rods Daddy offered him to use; he refused those. He had his own lunch, which was packaged in a Savannah sugar refinery's extra strength, long endurance bag, very popular in Savannah for all kinds of uses. Nonetheless, this old gentleman casually put something on his line as bait, lowered it over the side of the boat, and within minutes he was quietly pulling his rope up with not one, but two fish at a time. Maybe he was spraying something on the hook and the bait. Maybe he made it smellier than ours. Maybe he used bread dough and had a dead shrimp stuffed in the middle, which was a delicacy. Certainly it couldn't be because of his rig being a drop line.

I always marveled over that occurrence because it made me think of how much time rods and reels took to lug and oil them. More time was required to change the leads, set the drag, cast appropriately, not get tangled up, and have the right weight in sinkers. You also had to watch the tip of the rod to know the precise moment to set the hook or pull, based on the type of fish anticipated, and how quickly to reel in. Yet our senior citizen friend of the family would quietly drop a non-mechanical device with two hooks and seldom ever miss a fish or lose his bait.

When done for the day, we would have a half or close to a bushel of crabs and a mess of fish that Mama, in those days, didn't much mind cleaning or regard as a chore. And if we were really fortunate, we didn't use all of our good fresh shrimp, which also made for good eating when we returned home.

As we grew older, things improved a bit. We became the proud owners of a pink and gray Chris Craft 14-foot boat with a 35-horse-powered Evenrude & Johnson motor. It did not, however, have a dual-mode steering wheel, walk-around console, portable potty and musical radio. But this one had nicer seats with a place to put stuff and the anchor was stored out of the way in the hull. This pink and gray boat became a major attraction in our neighborhood and the source of self-invitation for newfound fishing friends. With this boat, it was a ceremony to go fishing.

It was also the source of newfound work in keeping it clean, draining and washing it out, which filled the rest of the twelve-hour day after we got home. A big water barrel in the back to rinse the salt water out of the engine was the "fun" part of the cleaning process. It was necessary to crank or pull the motor cord and start it up in the barrel, with water splashing all over and making a horrific noise.

As kids we even liked the noise and I'm sure this was much to the annoyance of all the neighbors.

This pink and gray boat was such a big deal in the Day family that on special days we all dressed in pink shirts and gray pants to grace the Wilmington River in our pink and gray boat. We always waved at passing boats no matter who was on them, and our pink and gray outfits upped the ante. While I do not think a name was painted on the boat, there was no doubt in my mind it was named "Laura Mae."

I recall many unfortunate situations but one was quite serious from my fishing memories. One day while quietly fishing in a cove, out of nowhere came a boat pulling a skier on a tether. My first thought was, and I'm sure Daddy's too, "This isn't good for fishing," and from the outset, it seemed a deliberate intrusion. We were sure of this when we saw the boat and the skier come close with broad smiles and waving only to make a complete turn and loop to spray us all with the water churned up from the skis. They were only eight to fifteen yards away from our boat. Daddy was a policeman and they had done something to offend us. At age eight or ten, it was clear to me, that this was grounds for arrest—that we should pull up anchors, track them down, handcuff and send them off to jail for a possibly long sentence. I could see Daddy pondering his action and I think he drew a line to give one time as a mistake and a second time as trouble. Fortunately, we never saw the second time.

On a more serious note, we were out near the mouth of the Atlantic Ocean, where ships from Savannah Ports and Savannahians have access to bigger waters for shipping, but also for fishing for bigger fish. Instead of settling for the Wilmington River, within minutes you could be at ocean side, at boat ramps, or near the jetties—with large brick barriers designed to limit shore erosion and break waves with high seas. The meeting of rivers with the Atlantic Ocean is where we would have a greater chance at snagging striped bass, tender hammer head, or shovel nose sharks, an occasional black drum, Spanish or king mackerel and even channel catfish and large Atlantic croakers. When caught, the fish were tremendous in size and fun to catch compared to river fishing.

We made all of the usual preparations that day, which included Daddy checking the weather. The day was sunny, but we would leave extremely early in the morning because it took a bit to get to the end of the jetties. We had signed in on the log, which was left in a mailbox type apparatus at the boat ramp. In our fourteen-foot Chris Craft boat, we drifted off course and within minutes the weather changed. We buttoned down tackle and rods and headed back—only to find we were running into even stronger waves, which initially were almost three feet high. This was tricky with a fourteen-foot boat, having to hit each wave head on and ride them in a manner that didn't cause the overflow to swamp the boat. This was made even more challenging with an outboard motor grinding up one side of the wave and racing down the other.

Before long, the waves had gained another foot or more in height, and sunny skies had completely succumbed to a dreary, overcast, and threatening-looking day. The contrast over a very short time as we continued to drift, was equivalent to driving a car through a dark tunnel after being on a sunny road for hours. Daddy was at the motor's handle and moved me into the center of the boat and my oldest brother into the front. As I looked over my shoulder and glanced into Daddy's face, it was clear to me the weather condition was serious business and what was a frightening situation had become one of survival. I did not see panic in Daddy's face, but a seriousness and intensity that's hard for a kid to forget because it was so different from his usual softer, more relaxed facial expressions. The next twenty minutes seemed like a lifetime in passing.

By the grace of God and I'm sure with a lot of silent praying by Daddy, and certainly by me, we finally saw the edge of the jetties, which might have been granite or gold as far as I was concerned. This meant we were close to a place with lower waves and the certainty of our rescue, should we capsize.

When we got back to the boat ramp, hauled the boat out of the water and headed home, we failed to make one important call. That was to Mama, to let her know we were okay. When we walked in and she saw that we were all uninjured and alive, she gave us a look as if she had decided it was okay to kill us herself–for making her worry, of course.

CHAPTER 12
THE CHECKER PLAYER, THE BILLIARDS POOL SHARK, AND THE MARKSMAN

Daddy worked six week rotating shifts. He didn't attend church with us. He did make time to do other things with us. When life was simpler in choices, governed principally by what you could afford, it was important to have enjoyable hobbies to offset work and pressures of everyday living. It was important to acquire a taste for sports where you could feel instant personal rewards, participate some with your children, and socialize with special friends. In our family and among friends, life's enjoyment meant more in the long run with the development of a close-knit relationship among us and with each individual son.

The passion for playing checkers is a favorite memory from the early '50s and '60s. Perhaps it was because it didn't take much to strike up a game. It was a great pastime to talk while playing and a crowd could easily congregate and see who was winning–or not. Our good friend Lawrence, from the Air Force, played a lot of checkers with us when Daddy was working and we learned quite a bit from him before he passed away.

Most checkerboards seemed to be homemade, often with a dark brownish background with green or black squares. The board was wide and long enough for two men to sit on milk cartons, corn bushels, or straight up chairs with the checkerboard stretched across their knees. Shady trees were good enough to set up; screened or unscreened porches would also do to strike up a good game.

The kind of talk you heard among men in those days was much like the barbershop conversation–razzing. The talk would be both about the game and the braggadocio of one's ability and how soon the game was going to be over. All this, while players would be commenting on the side about who was going to win the World Series, if Joe Louis was going to knock someone out in the first few rounds or if a black athlete would ever be able to play in historic Grayson Stadium where Babe Ruth played. (Note: Eventually "Shoeless" Joe Jackson, Jackie Robinson and Hank Aaron competed on this field).

In those days, the winning player would talk much trash and would do it with a gentle laugh. Talking trash in checkers was similar to the whist card player who turns the last trump card up with the plastic coating slapped on one's forehead. The card would hang there hands free for the opposing team to see who was going to win the game.

I never realized that Daddy could talk the talk. I knew that his partner at police work, James Nealy, and his best friend, Fess, along with other off-duty policemen that we all got to know, could really come up with some doozies that if you didn't know them would seem like a harsh put-down. But at home, Daddy was usually pretty stoic. The one time I remember him breaking out of character was when my brother was razzing me for having an ugly girlfriend. I replied, "It's not the beauty, it's the booty," and Daddy fell over laughing. But mostly, he was serious around us. What a revelation—Daddy could talk trash! He was fast and thoughtful, and he seemed to have a strategy of most chess players, looking a minimum of three or four moves ahead.

Checker games seemed short overall, but you couldn't just win one; you had to beat a guy three to five times in order to be convincing. As a result, checker games lasted for hours. I knew Daddy was good at checkers when his best friends and our extended families would always be egging him on for a quick game while visiting or passing by. We all came to like and enjoy checkers. (Gambling wasn't permitted on or off the premises of the Day family, but we cheated by using Ritz crackers with peanut butter or jelly on the top for betting, the wager for losing.) Checker playing was a very civil sport that could be found anywhere from 38th Street to Forsyth Park. In fact, it got so popular that the corner store that was run by Ms. Horstein was eventually changed over to become The Savannah Checkers Club. And even today, while it's moved to Martin Luther King Drive just north of where Susie and Jimmy's Rest Home used to be, there again is the new and well-attended checkers club.

This is where I went to conduct interviews for this book and research on Daddy. I found Al Clark, the rookie patrolman who worked with my father. I found James Wallace, a veteran policeman who has died since I had the pleasure of meeting and interviewing him. I met Ernest Maynor, a motorcycle policeman who still sports the bowlegs to go with it. I know James Nealy, my brother Robert's godfather and Daddy's first partner, would have been there too had he not passed on a few years earlier. I also know that John White would be there during the course of the day. It's not only a hangout, but a community center and news exchange forum, a support group, and a place where you could borrow a buck or two for a day or two. The new Savannah Checkers Club hasn't changed much from the old one on 39th and Burroughs Streets, one block from my house or from the porches and under trees all over town, particularly in the black community.

Billiards Pool

Pool tables were rare commodities. They were found in pool halls and where alcohol was served. There was a pool table in the police barracks annex, which was eventually made available to black officers. I don't recall ever seeing a pool table at anyone's home. Dr. Henry Collier, I recall, had one in the basement of his home near Mills B. Lane Parkway. So I'm not sure how Daddy got so good at it.

I can hear Daddy now, after reaming the third to the last ball to be played off of the table by using those infamous words, "Rack man, walk slow." In the old days there was a person (rack man) to rack your balls and collect a nickel tip for pulling the billiard balls out of the single leather pockets around each of the four corners and two sides (no ball return back then). I am told this too was a sport that Daddy liked and played well. He was a steady-handed shooter with a heavy stick and the ability to back a ball up or make it spin left or right and position a queue ball behind the next shot to be taken—unique skills, even before Minnesota Fats. Hitting the ball low and fast with a sharp jerk was enough to make it jump over one into another to avoid clearing the eight ball too soon. It does not surprise me that Daddy also did well in this sport because of his steady hands.

Target Shooting

All through his life these steady hands were blessings, not only in sports, but in mastering the weapon on which most police officers come to depend. Firearms were common around our house, from a police 38 special to an assortment of handguns and rifles, and even shotguns. But safety was always number one. They were never left exposed, always out of our reach, but immediately available to Daddy if there was a ruckus in the lane next to our house or across the street, or a neighbor calling for special police assistance. You see, a policeman is truly never off duty. Families who have a policeman at home all come to know this all too well.

Daddy spent considerable time on practice ranges. At any community contest he was considered a dead eye or straight shooter on demand. Former detective and city councilman and extended family member David Jones, puts it this way, "Your Daddy could shoot a carton of milk from under the arm of a running man."

When we were all younger, we would have shooting practice tests without bullets and targets, but with a dime sitting on a real gun to test and ensure our steadiness. The object was to aim, click and pull the trigger without the dime falling off. Mama wasn't a bad shot either. She was known as Queen of the Turkey Shoots in Hinesville, Georgia. She carried home edible prizes more often than not whenever there was a contest using a rifle to hit a bull's eye for free cakes, a bushel of greens or even a turkey. She would often come home with several. The question I have is how did she ever have time to keep that skill up and practice?

Daddy took guns seriously, accepted them as part of life, never left home without one, but was very cautious when it came to how firearms were used and stored. When we became young adults, Daddy said, "If you ever want a gun of your own, you're going to have to get it yourself." It was those words that brought the reality to me of what could happen to you with a gun as much as what you could do to someone else with a gun, self-defense or not. For this reason, I have managed to go without ever owning a gun!

CHAPTER 13
THE CIVIL RIGHTS MOVEMENT

In 1964 Martin Luther King, Jr. described Savannah as the most desegregated city south of the Mason-Dixon Line. This credit was given Savannah in part because of its comprehensive racial desegregation of public and private facilities starting in October 1963. This plan was some eight months ahead of the national Civil Rights Act. Savannah's forward thinking in this regard, with inclusion of blacks as part of the city's police force and other city government jobs, is believed to have also offset potential troubles involving violent acts and vandalism during the civil rights uprisings.

Savannah's participation in the civil rights movement was remarkably peaceful in the overall context of this country. However, the sit-in led by Dick Gregory at Burger Boy, an outdoor drive-in, and the Wade-In at Savannah

Beach (where blacks were not allowed) led by the Rev. Amos C. Brown and W. W. Law, had a profound effect on the community. The role of the local NAACP chapter in the lives of black Savannahians is also a story that remains largely untold by those who witnessed it first hand. This history of black Americans is far more important than stories of voodoo, walking imaginary dogs in Forsyth Park, transvestites, and doing the minuet at some mythical debutante ball.

Ballot Bus and "Trash"

The economic boycotts in Savannah extended from March 1960, to approximately October 1961, making it the first city in the state of Georgia with desegregated lunch counters. But not all lunch counters were desegregated in 1961. In February 1963, fifteen blacks, led by Dick Gregory, staged a sit-in at the Burger Boy Restaurant at 3810 Montgomery Street with an announcement that demonstrations would continue until they were served. The Burger Boy Restaurant was named in a suit in late 1964 and charged with violation of the 1964 Civil Rights Act.

Registration of some fifty percent of eligible black voters, which constituted one third of the city's population, played an important role in electing a moderate city government in the 1960s. W.W. Law was president of the Savannah branch of the NAACP beginning August 1955. Hosea Williams was head of the political arm of Savannah's NAACP. With the leadership of both men, voting power for blacks became a concern for city politicians. As a result, Malcolm McLean lived up to a campaign promise to fill one position with a black member to each council board.

Savannah's peaceful approach to the civil rights movement is credited in large part to local leaders not requiring outside assistance from larger national groups. It was only in 1963 that future Southern Christian Leadership Conference colleagues joined the local protest rather than directing it. The mood of the civil rights leaders in Savannah was always to keep the commercial boycotts and other demonstrations among Savannahians and to avoid "bringing Martin Luther King to the city."

While W.W. Law headed the NAACP and Hosea Williams served as Vice President, they were also responsible for a number of other locally known activists becoming colleagues of Martin Luther King and the larger southeastern civil rights movement. These included Benjamin Van Clark, James Brown, and Willie Bolden, all of whom became field workers associated with SCLC (The Southern Christian Leadership Conference) in Savannah.

Savannah used techniques for demonstrations similar to those used in Atlanta and other cities: mass meetings at churches, wade-ins at beaches, and ride-ins on the buses. In fact, Judson Ford claimed to lead the first unofficial "piss-in" demonstrations using segregated restrooms. Black leadership in Savannah called for a complete economic boycott of the downtown area until charges were dropped against the students who were conducting the first sit-ins. The demands also included higher-ranking jobs for blacks in city government as well as those in stores, and the use of "courtesy titles" for black customers. During the '61 to '63 time frame, boycotts were also effective in gaining access to libraries, golf courses, parks, airports, and eating areas at bus stations as well as the hiring of other targeted positions such as firemen. While movie theaters were on the list with a commitment by city officials in June 1963 to become integrated, this promise was reneged on repeatedly. It was a hot and confrontational summer with several cases of random or negligent violence.

In the 1960s, Savannah's population was near 150,000, with approximately 36 percent of the inhabitants classified as Negroes. By comparison to other similarly sized southern cities, Savannah's blacks were considerably behind their white counterparts economically. They held a larger percentage of laborer jobs and earned approximately one-third of the income of whites. Housing conditions in the black community typified the economic divide. Savannah, however, escaped the vindictive race relationships more typical of the south during the civil rights movement.

Leaders such as former attorney and then Judge Eugene Gadsden; NAACP president W.W. Law; Drs. Henry Collier, Jr. and John William Jamerson, Jr. were among civil rights leaders who helped ensure Savannah's mild, but successful, civil rights experience. This was also attributed to the openness of leaders on both sides and ongoing discussions during the ordeals. The more liberal outlook in the community was also inherited from Savannah's proximity to an open coastline and its seaport orientation with associated trade. The transient nature of Savannah gave its residents the opportunity to see many different people, nationalities and cultures in and out of the city over an extended period of time.

The *New York Times* reported that the business community in Savannah in the 1963 time period saw fit to end strife through negotiations, thus heading off even more extensive uprisings. Overall it was concluded that the Negro sections of Savannah were better off than neighboring rural communities in southwestern Georgia and other southern cities, which experienced greater disturbances.

The Rev. Ralph Mark Gilbert and his legacy are credited with galvanizing non-violent ideals and deep penetration into the Savannah black community. However, active leaders such as Benjamin Van Clark and W.W. Law made no mistake about the existence of racism toward blacks in Savannah during the civil rights era. Both commented specifically on tokenism and confrontations with blacks. W.W. Law was targeted and removed from his postal job with an obscure complaint, probably due to his leadership in the NAACP.

The nonviolent downtown business district boycott lasted for some eighteen months. It had a significant impact and led to local government negotiations with the NAACP leaders. W.W. Law stands out among all during that era, perhaps as the most influential local civil rights leader in the entire south. Under his leadership, Savannah was credited with having the most organized initiatives in the NAACP efforts in Savannah.

The Rev. Lewis Steele oversaw the area of integrated education. Mercedes Wright chaired the Boycott Committee, and Curtis Cooper was responsible for Youth Council and Development. Carolyn Quilloin led the ride-ins and Deacon Winters was in charge of membership drives. The efforts of Hosea Williams and later Eugene Gadsden contributed significantly to the achievements in voter registration. Of course lots of help came from folks like Big Lester and Trash (Henry "Trash" Brown Lee) recruiting longshoremen from union halls to vote and to be part of the protest movement. Credit is also given to Monsignor John D. Toomey, who also received credit as the chief facilitator of talks between white and black negotiators. This enabled negotiated decisions, in the form of a truce, to be reached in December 1963. There are other heroes and significant figures who played a major part in bringing about change in Savannah.

Big Lester and "Trash" Recruiting Longshoremen

Voter registration was and continues to be a banner objective for the NAACP and civil rights causes. With inclusion of voter registration as a priority in Savannah, the formation of a Chatham County Crusade for Voters (CCCV), an arm of the NAACP led by Hosea Williams, gave new credibility among middle class blacks for the overall objective and processes for bringing about change. People like Lester Hankerson stood out in the Savannah black community as part of a grassroots operation for recruiting folks to vote from street corners, union halls and taverns. The ballot bus was a visible sign of the voter registration drive. It was an older model sedan that was driven through the neighborhoods with painted writing that read: "Free rides, no excuses."

Dr. Henry M. Collier Counting Contributions

People like James C. Middleton, Sr. and Willie Mae Aiken were among those who assisted the voter registration movement. Dr. Henry M. Collier, Jr. noted that the many stumbling blocks for registering voters included literacy tests and poll taxes. Curtis Cooper recalled that in addition to the ballot bus, that local organizers used a mule with a sign saying, "I'm not registered because I am a "jackass" (in picture form). What's your excuse?" The NAACP and the SCLC had to rely on men like Hosea Williams and Benjamin Van Clark for grassroots activities. This effort, plus others by the NAACP and Martin Luther King, Jr., was acknowledged by Andrew Young to be specifically targeted for publicity against injustice. People like Carolyn Roberts Barlow staffed an office donated by the Mine, Mill and Smelters Workers Union.

In 1962 a massive voter registration campaign culminated with some 17,000 black residents becoming eligible to vote. This was significant since it overcame drawbacks and literacy tests that accompanied rulings and ordinances of 1948 for open registrations.

Ironically, the Chatham County Crusade for Voters (CCCV) ended up in somewhat of a competing position with the main NAACP organization and organized more aggressive protests, including night marches in the summer of 1963. Ultimately, the broader support and backing of the principal NAACP organization was such that Hosea Williams ended up leaving Savannah and the CCCV organization to join the Southern Christian Leadership Conference in Atlanta.

Many who attended the mass meetings in the evenings at theaters or churches described the experience of passing a basket for depositing weapons, or anything that could be construed as such, on a table before going out that night for a march. Things such as brass knuckles, switchblades, pocket knives, or anything that could be considered a weapon would be a basis for added trouble in the event of being accosted or arrested.

Hosea Williams Preaching, Tomochichi Rock in Wright Square

Marches

The civil rights movement in Savannah was probably at its peak in the summer of 1963 when afternoon and night marches took place. Still fuming from an incident with Levy's Department Store, several black youths were arrested, and a boycott of Broughton Street followed. Stores such as Kress, Woolworth's and McCrory's were all on the target list for sit-ins. The lunch counter "Closed" signs didn't stop the Savannah protesters. Neither did, in some cases, being spat upon or physically assaulted by passersby, who seemingly were never apprehended. The nonviolent approach was not easy.

My brother and I did not march in the civil rights movement because Daddy didn't want to find himself in the position of having to arrest us. I graduated from high school in 1962 and was in college before the movement really began heating up. Daddy was a patrolling policeman and part of his job was to arrest people who were demonstrating inappropriately. Even though he would lose favor with close friends, Daddy was part of the system.

I also remember a big struggle in words between NAACP head W. W. Law, who delivered mail to our house and Daddy. I overheard conversations when Mr. Law wanted to convince Daddy to get more involved. I think he may have been a member but didn't want to attend the meetings. I'm sure other black policemen handled it differently, but Daddy wasn't about to be seen at a mass meeting then the next day arrest people for demonstrating. There was pressure put on him to conform. "You yourself are experiencing discrimination," they would tell him. But he never became publicly involved with the movement.

While police often were left to interpret "anti-trespass law," this offered no consolation to those who would likely be arrested if they did not leave the premises when asked to by the proprietor of a business. Some of the protestors paid tribute to officers such as David Jones, who had a more calming influence on crowds. Other protestors felt that black officers were only called to a scene when it became necessary to remove them from the premises for jailing.

Hosea Williams was known to use the Tomochichi Rock named for the Yamacraw leader, during lunchtime to speak to a crowd of civil rights protestors until one day he was asked directly by Sydney B. Barnes, Chief of Police, to come down off of the Tomochichi's Rock at Wright Square or be arrested. Hosea complied. Morrison's Cafeteria, not far from City Hall, was another targeted place for sit-ins that refused service to blacks. Demonstrations in Savannah, as in other civil rights movements, used the songs like "Ain't Nobody Gonna Turn Us Round" and "We Shall Overcome" as the main motivating pieces to get protestors spirited about their assignments. Then City Manager, A.A. (Don) Mendonsa, was said to be present during the civil rights marches, often accompanied by city attorney James B. Blackburn.

Savannah is believed to be the first city to initiate night marches. There was great concern by organizers at first regarding added dangers for being struck by flying objects and the like, but overall the marches attracted a larger crowd after school and normal business hours. There was, of course, fear that tagalongs, particularly those who used alcohol beforehand, would jeopardize safety.

Chief of City Police Sydney B. Barnes spoke to the issue as to whether the police department would use dogs, and he vehemently stated that it was absolutely not an option. While dogs had a psychological effect, they were mainly included on the police force for apprehension during burglaries and other crimes. There were no reports of dog attacks in the Savannah civil rights movement.

Getting Arrested

The natural occurrence and result of the day and night marches in Savannah was incarceration of many for obstruction, loitering, and occasional trespassing. Sitting in and picketing inappropriately were other bases for arrest. Many of the protestors and marchers had different experiences as far as being jailed. They were often separated in different facilities across town and of course separated by race and sex. Many complained about the crowded conditions, the stench, lack of light, and quality of air as well as just sheer fear of what could happen at any minute. Some noted that they would be released in the middle of the night without any means of transportation and have to walk long distances in the street to get home. This in itself was viewed as a potential punishment for those arrested. A number of the marchers felt it was an honor to go to jail and actually ran for the paddy wagon in order to be able to say that they in fact had proved their dedication and fearlessness in the cause.

Peace bonds and other deeds on property were often brought in to get the arrested freed. Not only did the leaders like Benjamin Clark and Hosea Williams spend time in jail, but Andrew Young was also with them on occasions. There are some reports of lengthy imprisonments, but most seemed to be in just a day or two, only to return to other sit-ins and demonstrations. Having overrun the city police holding area on Habersham Street, and other facilities, including Travis Field, and other military facilities, were used for a large number of prisoners. There are several reports of guard hostility while in jail; however, there were few official charges of any brutality by guards. There are reports that athletes as well as student councils from the various schools were well represented during the sit-ins and in the jailing. The Reverend Frank Ellis reports, however, that the impact of imprisonment was so great psychologically that when he was released, he reported that he would do anything for the movement except go to jail.

Protestor Support

While many students and young people constituted the greater percentage of marchers day and night, there was remarkable support for the movement at all levels in the black community and among some white civil rights activists. The attendance of the young people at demonstrations worried parents substantially and caused students to participate reluctantly if, in fact, permission was granted.

For the older supporters, including teachers and government workers, it was not uncommon that financial support and other in-kind contributions were made quietly to avoid being targeted for job dismissal. Private businessmen, physicians, lawyers, funeral directors, and ministers had greater independence of the "system" and could more openly show support. Dr. Henry M. Collier, Jr., for example, was seen helping to count donations and in other ways assisting with menial labor chores, as well as, I'm sure, providing significant financial contribution himself. The use of churches and black radio stations for the voter registration drive and for appearances by local civil rights leaders provided another good measure of community support.

Desegregation Negotiated

Through all the voter registration drives, sit-ins, marches, the organizing of people of conscience, Savannah achieved an end to racial segregation through negotiations. The real mark of distinction for Savannah is that it managed to reach this point ahead of the congressional act of 1964, with the Civil Rights Bill. Savannah came through the summer of 1963, reached a point of settlement with city leaders and businessmen, and began a new chapter with respect to racial acceptance and desegregation.

It took business leaders, black and white, government officials, and church ministers to bring about this miraculous accomplishment. In fact, there was a committee of 100 businesses in Savannah and the Toomey Committee that helped pull things together. Judge Eugene Gadsden and W. W. Law are still mentioned in writings about the ending of the struggles throughout the civil rights movement, the settlement, and the continuing effort to preserve equality among all. Agreements were being reached with the Blue Ribbon committee and even after some agreements were reached, some marching still ensued. Many meetings took place at the Flamingo Club on Gwinnett Street.

Some commented that the civil rights movement in Savannah was fortunate not to have an opposing organization of whites to counteract and to complicate the efforts for equality in the city. There were many testimonies about the influence of the Ku Klux Klan with telephone calls about running folks off the road and picketing in certain areas. While the Klan made its mark, it never reached a point of turning the black civil rights movement around from ultimate negotiations in the summer of 1963.

Savannah is credited with a number of other factors that were coincidental to the successful non-violent movement in comparison to other cities in the country. These included a moderate mayor, leadership and discipline in the Savannah Police Department, which had already begun integration in 1947, and great determination by community leaders to do what it took to keep the city intact. Mayor McLean and City Manager Medonsa were open enough to accept community leaders and kept communications open during all of the civil rights movement.

Savannah was blessed with active grassroots campaigns organized by day-to-day people who saw the need and rose to the challenge to do something to make a difference, beginning with voter registration into marches, sit-ins and other protests. The strong leadership of the NAACP and Chatham County Crusade for Voters' efforts were well organized and protest participants were, overall, well handled, instructed and monitored. The awareness of business community members and professionals who saw the need and supported it directly and indirectly made a significant difference. Perhaps the number of these individual black leaders and ministers was equivalent to other southern cities. The percent of activism among them must have been greater. In the end, the settlement for peaceful accord was a testimony that all sides had a vested interest of equal proportion and incentive to keep the city intact, share more of its resources, and begin to look at each other differently and closer as neighbors, rather than servants. Savannah's early inclusion of black police officers and other workers as city employees undoubtedly contributed significantly to a rather peaceful outcome and forward thinking.

CHAPTER 14
THE SHOOTING

It was a day in January 1963, which promised to be a normal day in the life of Savannah during the civil rights movement. Three years earlier, local sit-ins that began with Dick Gregory had started a new era and pattern of demonstrations in Savannah. Mass demonstrations and a boycott of Broughton Street merchants periodically created packed streets of students, adult demonstrators, onlookers, and a smattering of tagalong troublemakers.

Daddy was regularly assigned in the area of West Broad Street between the Star Theater and Council's Lounge near the YMCA at the corner of West Broad (now MLK, Jr. Blvd.) and Gwinnett Streets. On that January day from 3:00 to 5:00 p.m., he was accompanied by a new police recruit, Albert Clark. This location was the end point for daily marches organized by Hosea Williams, W.W. Law,

Curtis Cooper, and a host of other Savannah civil rights activists.

The marches started on East Broad Street at approximately 3:00 p.m. after the students, who constituted the bulk of demonstrators, were out of school. They would assemble at a church on East Broad Street near Gwinnett, a predominately black section, and be given instructions along with a brief prayer service. These daily marches would proceed north on East Broad, west on Broughton and south on West Broad Street. This particular day, the marches were coming to an end near Gwinnett and West Broad Streets where Daddy and Officer Clark were patrolling the streets. As usual, the crowd was at its peak. Near the end of the march, just before disbanding, demonstrators became louder and more boisterous. By the time they reached West Broad and Gwinnett, a number of older adults, tagalongs and rabble-rousers had joined in.

Daddy had often met the challenge facing black police officers in situations of patrolling a predominantly black section of town. Officers were taught to avoid taking issue with the rights of the marchers and their cause. Sometimes hecklers in the crowd shouted jeers and abuse at the officers who were trying to quiet the crowd in an orderly manner and have them disperse as quickly as possible without incident. While most respected the black policemen, there were those who viewed them as being puppets of the white establishment and made them targets for ridicule, particularly in association with the marchers. This particular evening, a small crowd refused to disband at the end of the day's march. Many adults had flocked to the streets from nearby bars and saloons and were beginning to congregate on sidewalks outside of storefront businesses, lingering in the street and blocking traffic. An older man who had been drinking began shouting obscenities and attempting to incite the remaining crowd the police were attempting to disband. The officers became the target of this citizen's obscenities.

Daddy firmly worked to quiet the heckler and move him along out of the area. However, after being told repeatedly to calm down, move along, and cease the disturbance, Mr. Harold Jones began directing his obscenities at Daddy. A few of the remaining spectators viciously egged Mr. Jones on in his remarks of disrespect, which escalated to comments that he would "take anyone out who tried to stop him from expressing his views." While Daddy continued attempts to reduce the tension and convince the crowd that they should move on without incident, Mr. Jones began threatening that he was armed and meant business.

It was about this time that the new police recruit, Albert Clark, entered the fracas. Previous employment with the city of Savannah as a Public Housing Department maintenance supervisor and a union representative had made Officer

Clark familiar with many of the street folks who tagged along with the civil rights marchers. His manner with them was therefore notably different from my father's.

Unfortunately, the well-intentioned intervention by Officer Clark had an opposite effect. His direct talk and demanding tone escalated tensions. Black officers had received specific training for dealing with civil rights demonstrators. Officer Clark's manner and relationship with those who were still mingling in the street eventually led to a showdown between Harold Jones and my father. With his hand in his pocket, Mr. Jones implied that he was there to stay, was unwilling to move, and would "take no shit." At this point, many of the civil rights marchers scrambled for safety and left the scene. But a number of the more seasoned locals remained behind to see what would happen. As Mr. Jones reached into his pocket and moving forward as if pulling a gun, he was shot by my father. I would imagine Mr. Jones' threats ring true in my mind.

Daddy was known to be one of the best shots in the Police Department. Was it the instinct of a marksman to shoot to kill, rather than disable Mr. Jones? We will never know. My father would not ever discuss it with us. But at about 4:53 p.m., January 16, 1963, a single shot took Mr. Jones' life and forever changed Daddy's life—and the lives of two families.

All street noise came to a dead silence. Witnesses from barbershops and salons stood still as Daddy radioed for an ambulance and backup support in the event there would be additional reaction by the remaining crowd. In seconds, West Broad Street was screaming with sirens and glittering with flashing police lights and an emergency ambulance. For Mr. Jones, it was too late–he had died instantly.

What happened next is standard procedure in police business. The reports were written. Fellow officers escorted Daddy back to the barracks; assisting officers and some witnesses were interviewed. At the end of the shift, Daddy was relieved of his service revolver and placed on leave pending a full investigation. It was close to 10:00 p.m. when Sgt. John A. White, the highest ranking black police officer at that time and several other police officers escorted Daddy home.

My mother received the call that Daddy was coming home early from his shift because something had happened. As a policeman's wife she must have always lived with imagining the risks he was facing. But this call was for real. I could tell from the expression on Mama's face that she didn't know the details and this was not good.

My brothers and I were completely shocked to have so many squad cars delivering our father home. Comments from policemen escorting Daddy, all with good intentions, included, "Things will work out." "It's going to be okay."

"Keep the faith," and "We will patrol regularly as long as it takes until this flies over." But not one of them explained what had happened or how it happened.

One of the most dreaded of all events in a policeman's career is to have to draw his revolver, particularly under the threat of being shot by an assailant. The emotions surrounding split-second decisions are hard to explain, but can change the lives of many family members, cause lengthy scrutiny of judgment and actions and impact an entire career and lifetime. When a police shooting occurs during a face-off resulting in the loss of a civilian's life, the consequence looms large within a small community and in the relationships of policemen involved.

It is common for a police officer to be immediately suspended after a shooting with time off work both to pull himself together and give internal affairs an opportunity to investigate. When Daddy arrived home, he was escorted by several patrol cars and they continued to patrol closely in the neighborhood in the first few days afterwards, presumably to protect him from harm or revenge. This entire time was frightening to us. I did not get a clear-cut story then and had to research for this book exactly what happened. My brothers and I wanted to ask what was happening and I was usually the one to dare to speak up and create a scene with my questions. This, however, wasn't one of those times. We all remained silent.

Never before had I seen such distress on Daddy's face. I saw sadness, remorse, shock, anger, bewilderment, and worry. Yet he was seemingly vigilant with increased sensitivity about all that happened around him. Small noises, which used to come and go unnoticed, created more intensive alarm and awareness. Movements outside with car noises or people caused more response initially. But more importantly was the somber and quiet moments of knowing he was in the next room and knowing that he was not asleep. There is absolutely nothing a child can do but stay out of the way. Mama was able to reach deeply to comfort him, console him on his decision to shoot, and otherwise support him as still being the man that she knew and loved. I only figured this out by how she cooked, talked, and acted for the next several weeks until the hearing acquitted him and he was back on the beat again.

The days and weeks following created a changed relationship between Daddy and his comrades in the police department and perhaps with the city as a whole. This is not to exclude the effect on family members in a town as small as Savannah, then about 200,000 people. The nature of life changed for the Day family in many ways, but surely not as significantly as for the family of Harold Jones.

I felt heightened concern for actions of revenge, even though I was in college locally at Savannah State University. In travel to nighttime jobs at Hester's Restaurant, the

Savannah Yacht and Country Club, and the DeSoto Hilton Hotel, I wondered if my brother or I would face a family member of the deceased trying to make things even. I also feared that sniper shots might be taken at my father at work or even while off duty. At school things were considerably more peaceful, since a large number of the students were not from Savannah and possibly did not know the particulars of the incident.

Because this incident was associated with the civil rights march, a good cause, and with a black police officer and a black victim with black families, a myriad of questions were forever raised.

Why did it happen?

Daddy must have thought about this moment hundreds of times.

Other officers must have asked, "What would I have done? How would I deal with the pressure of such a moment?"

Our family asked, "What can we do for our father?

What is the price he'll pay?

What will happen to our family?

Why wasn't additional reinforcement called for before the incident occurred and why would the crowd, after knowing the difficult position of police and blacks in our own neighborhoods, egg things on?"

If this had happened thirty years later, no doubt someone would have caught the incident on video. But we were not so fortunate and questions still linger today. When I attempted to interview Officer Albert Clark for this book, he said that he promised he would never discuss it, so these questions remain unanswered. A couple of weeks later, following the official investigation and hearings, Daddy was eventually reinstated to duty, but life would not be quite the same. As a patrolman, a fellow officer, a black citizen, a father, a husband, and a buddy's friend, there were dozens who were touched by this officer's life and his continuing dedication to the work of policing our community.

Mama's attention to Daddy's travel time to and from work was even more exacting. She wanted to know more about the overtime hours, patrolling ballparks and the like, and kept pretty good tabs on Daddy's whereabouts on and off duty. She also was supportive in her mannerism with even greater care in her voice in general conversations, about keeping house, preparing timely meals, and helping to get him out to work–things some modern women would feel are outdated–but, my parents worked it out.

I noticed an even more serious and pensive demeanor about Daddy following the shooting which demonstrated a lot of remorse and regret–more so than fear. To say he became a kinder and gentler person would overstate his professional demeanor when going to work and doing his job. I believe he also knew it would forever affect his career progress, perceptions in the community, and how his fellow officers and peers viewed him.

Over the years, I've noticed at policemen's retirements and in other readings about police life, the recognition of the pressures of public scrutiny and the strain on marriages and children. I've also come to notice that at the point of retirement, those officers who never had to use their revolvers in the line of duty receive special acknowledgement for that. In fact, it seems to be a heralded position to not have fired your gun while on duty. With detailed training and preparation for this type of situation, one might come to think that all complex shooting situations and face-offs should be resolved without shooting. A police officer may find him or herself in a real life-threatening situation and thrust into a "shoot, don't-shoot" decision in a matter of seconds and with practically no notice. And yet police shootings continue to occur with the same devastating impact felt in Savannah and in our home.

A few weeks before the shooting and while coaching Albert Clark, the new recruit, the two were summoned to a citizen's home where there was a person or animal on the front porch trying to get in. This night, they discovered that it was an opossum rather than a villain that caused the call for police assistance. Daddy, described by former policeman David Jones as capable of "shooting a milk carton from under the arms of a running man," chose not to shoot on this occasion. Instead, he insisted on coming up with ways to release it back into the wild without taking its life.

A sad aspect of a policeman's life is that the term "off-duty policeman" is an oxymoron because a policeman is never "off duty" whether out of uniform, shopping, taking a stroll, or watching a kid's football game.

The sadness of their families when an officer takes a life goes on forever. It also colors the attitude of the officer and the family toward this job as an officer. No matter the circumstances, he will feel regret and will begin to second- guess his actions. But he will always seem to stay more finely attuned to the next potential crisis as he will scrutinize his decisions even more closely. Will he likely take three to four more seconds to assess the appropriateness of an action, and will the extra time be too long for his own safety and potentially that of others? In police codes, an officer down or in trouble, a shooting, or gang action against one or two policemen are still the most urgent calls police departments nationwide respond to with force. In a very real sense, Officer Day was down after this shooting, but there was no police code for that.

CHAPTER 15

THE CHANGE IN PRIORITIES

Life as usual returned after some months. Daddy continued his shifts, five days working, one resting, one fishing or breaking away to play checkers. There was always something to fiddle with in our house, and one repair would lead to another. The next year, in 1964, Bill my older brother, (known during those days as Billy) married. Three years later I left for graduate school. Edmund was placed in an institution around that time. I got married in '69. This was the first big deal church wedding we all attended as a family, and it meant a lot to my parents to see their boys start their lives. Robert was still at home and—unlike Bill and me—attending a Catholic school. That was an advantage of being the last one at home. The disadvantage was that Daddy was older and not playing ball as much with him, as he had with us.

After working for some twenty-five years as a policeman at the rank of Private First Class, my father had become resigned to the fact that he would never be promoted. It must have become clear after the first five years, when he turned forty, that being promoted was not necessarily in the cards for him.

He had completed a degree at Savannah State College, then called Georgia State College. There were only three cadets who attended college in the first class of black police officers, and only one out of the three (Daddy) secured a degree. There was great emphasis, however, on military background as a prerequisite for hiring and promotions in government-related positions. Daddy's work as a truant officer, teacher, and school bus driver helped, but did not equal the training by some who were formerly soldiers and marines. This is why Daddy was the tenth man, rather than one of the original nine. Fellow officer John White was one of the first black marines and later became a sergeant on the police force. Daddy's partner, James Nealy was a military policeman in the service but never received a promotion on the police force.

Lieutenant John White

The problem, as I can best determine, was that Daddy was older than most of the new recruits. He had more experience with life than most black and white officers, and Daddy had developed a personality as "being his own man." He was not willing to blindly take orders or carry out missions based on vague instructions, but rather questioned his superiors for clarity. He was intolerant of political favoritism and unfair criticism. Officer William Malone attested to this stating "Your Daddy didn't just take stuff." What he referred to on several occasions was the attitude and behavior of white officers who humiliated or put down the black officers. This was often done by "poking fun," mocking or chastising black officers for every little incident or characteristic. Once again, Daddy's extremely light complexion was the primary target for many white officers, who disrespectfully drew the conclusion about his racially mixed parentage.

"Hey—what white guy made you from your mama?"

"Hey, my mother was white," he'd answer without missing a beat.

Several of the "Original Nine" and other black officers on the police force told me that Daddy would set it straight and without hesitation, no matter who offered a derogatory comment with respect to his parents, their aptitudes, or their abilities.

For some officers, skin color wasn't the issue. Their height, manner of speech, level of literacy or, often, a basic misunderstanding of police protocol would become their source of humiliation. There were also those, I'm, told, who played the political and social game very well. In fact, one or two even went so far as to serve as a pipeline from Waldburg Street (the black precinct) to Oglethorpe Street (the main headquarters). These pipeline reports, made by black officers to white administrators, were about issues of complaints by other black officers, their peers. This communication continued even after they were moved to the main headquarters. Some of the exposed grievances were of a magnitude that meetings were arranged to discuss them. Some even culminated with formal hearings.

Some from the original group, however, decided to strike out on their own and get out from under the politics of police business. Frank Mullino left the police department and became a merchant marine, which in the late '40s and '50s was one of the most lucrative jobs available. Milton Hall, who rode a nice looking motorcycle to and from work, left to start the Milton Cab Company and other businesses.

Daddy, on the other hand, was extremely committed to his position as a police officer and to the city of Savannah. So instead of his promotion and advancement, he made it a priority to help other black officers get ahead in the profession. He mentored new recruits such as Lucius "Bo"

Levett, Ernest Maynor, and a host of others. He assisted some of the early officers who struggled with completing police reports properly, including his partner James Nealy.

Accepting one's fate of no further advancement in your chosen career must be difficult to deal with. Dealing with it proudly and constructively has got to be even more challenging. That's the legacy Daddy left with his sons. It's interesting to observe how some of Daddy's personality traits and characteristics run so deeply in our family. Without exception, each son has faced critical job decisions, oftentimes similar to what it must have been like at the Savannah Police Department. In each case we resorted to different alternatives, including sticking it out, moving laterally, and just deciding at the appropriate moment to leave. This is what I did. I left my executive level job with a well known airline to start a consulting business. In all cases, the characteristic of feeling good about speaking our mind, being respectful to others, and not being caught up into other folks' power plays seems to be a common thread in the Day family.

With health problems becoming more acute during the later years of police work, Daddy set his sights on retirement by sixty-two or sixty-five years old. His interest grew stronger in better equipping family members and helping them with options for success. For one thing, he was determined that everyone would finish college. He would live long enough to see a daughter and two sons graduate prior to marriage, as well as an eighteen-year-old son in private school who later completed college. I remember conversations about the importance of preparing yourself to be a school teacher in addition to whatever other course work you would pursue for other careers.

Bill, my older brother, and I were mathematics majors, but we both minored in education with the idea that no matter what other occupations we considered, we would benefit from teaching skills and be prepared to enter the highly respected career of teaching school. We both finished Savannah State College with teaching certificates and completed practice teaching.

In fact, William Jr. (Bill) started his career as a math teacher locally at Sol Johnson High School. Later he pursued a federal government career with the Job Corps Program as a teacher and counselor in California, Ohio, Minnesota and Missouri.

He was Director of Weber Basin Job Corps Center in Ogden, Utah. He transferred to US Department of Labor's Job Corps Regional Office as project manager for the Atlanta Job Corps Center. In 1977 he was promoted to Director, Office of Youth Programs, US Department of Interior, where he was responsible for Job Corps Centers, Young Adult Conservation Corps (YACC) and Youth Conservation Corps (YCC) in eight southeastern states, the Virgin Islands and

Puerto Rico. In 1984, he transferred to the US Department of Commerce, Economic Development Administration and served as Economic Development Representative and Chief of Business Loans, and in 1995, Commerce Secretary Ronald H. Brown appointed him as Regional Director of the Economic Development Administration and he was inducted into the Senior Executive Service (SES).

Bill retired after 38 years of federal service and serves on several boards of directors as well as being the Senior Warden of the Episcopal Church of the Holy Cross in Decatur, Georgia. He is Broker of his own real estate firm in the Atlanta area. Bill fulfilled Daddy's dream for him in building a family, being responsible, and earning a decent and honest living.

My younger brother, Robert, has work experience more closely aligned to Daddy's in working at the U.S. Postal Service. As a supervisor, he sees the ins and outs of day-to-day struggles of just breaking even. He finished Savannah State College with a degree in business administration and became employed as an accountant for a local manufacturing firm while pursuing several different positions, including shift work at the U.S. Postal Service. This parallels in some ways what Daddy's life as a local city government worker must have been like.

I recall how I made my decision at the end of high school about which college to attend. I had been scouted for basketball and football by several Georgia schools as well as Oklahoma State University. Daddy's comment was, "You can decide wherever you'd like to go, but remember one thing. If you attend Savannah State, you will always have a meal." I never forgot that statement, and when looking at grants offered from Savannah State versus other schools, and considering the requirement to play two sports from the same scholarship at other universities, it was clear to me that I was a hometown-bound college freshman waiting to happen.

By attending college at home, we spent more time together as a family, enlightening time with our parents, which we would especially appreciate later on. The decision to remain in Savannah and excel academically and in sports while maintaining part-time jobs was an education in itself.

Leaving a tight-knit family, even at twenty-two was traumatic. Going off in a borrowed '55 Buick to Southern Illinois University in Carbondale, Illinois, to become a teaching assistant and pursue graduate work in mathematics was no small deal for me.

Going from a school environment in a town of 200,000 and a school of 2,000 to a town with a population of 8,000 and a university of 25,000 in the Midwest was a frightening experience. After struggling with the social change, low funds, and realizing that pure mathematics, versus applied, was not as much fun as I thought, it was time to move on. It did not help that the department heads felt a change from one area to the other was an annoyance to their outside recruitment program. But I changed into applied mathematics anyway.

Recognizing the importance of having full-time work while pursuing a graduate degree, I seized an opportunity to become a mathematician at the U.S. Navy Yard in Washington, D.C. The job was defense-security related and also provided civilian support for the Vietnam War and related defense from "homeland security" threats (long before there was a Homeland Security Department). This also constituted a deferment for many, but being asthmatic, I was unable to pass a physical to enlist–even if it was what I wanted to do, which I didn't.

Prior to landing that job, one of my college professors at Savannah State, Mrs. Joan Gordon, advised me to stay in touch with the school, and she further recommended that while in Washington, D.C., I should visit with her son, Asa Gordon, meet his wife, Carol, and be sure to ask Carol about her sister. I followed Dr. Gordon's recommendations and Joy ultimately became my wife for thirty-five years.

Ironically, Daddy was concerned that my defense intelligence position was like the FBI or law enforcement. It seems as if Daddy was steering me away from a kind of job he thought would put me into harm's way and an experience that might include some of the pressures and difficulties he had personally endured. I recall that when I assumed the position at the U.S. Navy Yard, it required a top-secret clearance, including a hometown background check with government clearance officers visiting neighbors. I think all of the neighbors who were contacted about what I was like and if I was a clean-cut all-American kid probably thought I had committed some horrendous crime and was in serious trouble—especially with the agents coming from Washington, D.C. Word got back to my family as quickly as neighbors were contacted, as they all wanted to know how Charles was doing in Washington. In fact, it was difficult to convince my future bride that I was not a sailor but worked in the U.S. Navy Yard and I had a legitimate civilian job involving mathematics and orbital analysis.

As I think back, my folks' decision to pay close attention to preparing us was so genuinely unselfish. They must have set aside many of their own desires to muster funds to take care of a family the size of ours. Balancing the care of an invalad child and all of our many activities took an experienced juggler to manage. There was never ever a school event, a performance or trip or new outfit that I really needed that was not provided for me. In fact, one of the most revealing and kindest things I had ever said to Daddy is that I thought we were rich when I was growing up. Considering we owned a four-flat home and rented three of the four units, its no wonder I felt we were rich. I still feel the closeness of family life in Savannah with the type of parents who didn't appear to sacrifice at all, but made things happen that included their kids. They spent time preparing us to become productive citizens with good jobs. Being responsible, educated, not being taken advantage of by the "system," and having a decent and respectable job—this was all important to them, a good and essential responsibility met.

I recall that my parents demonstrated a genuine interest in improving life for everyone. My parents also provided for Patsy, our half sister, Daddy's daughter from a pre-marriage relationship. While Patsy was a young adult, she needed a place to live and 2204 Burroughs Street was cleared for her use. I'm pretty sure the unit was rented free or for a nominal amount to Patsy. I know this must have been difficult for my Mama to live with gossip, and challenging for both parents. But somehow they dealt with the situation in a manner that makes me proud of them. Assistance to Patsy enabled her to get back on her feet. Patsy was sixteen years my senior and I really regret not spending more time over the years to really get to know her. It would have also been nice to know what growing up with a sister was really like.

I think back to all of the major events that my brothers and I experienced in life which ultimately involved our parents. Whether it was graduation, award ceremonies, speaker at a special assembly, big athletic games, or escort for a class queen, somehow one and occasionally both of my parents managed to be there. But even at football games, if Daddy was on shift, in uniform, I could count on his assignment being arranged so that he could see the game and I could see my father cheering on the sideline, often in uniform if not off duty. He was also one of my greatest coaches with respect to personal conduct. I recall at a basketball tournament game at St. Pius, being frustrated and slapping the floor because I thought a referee had made a bad call. That behavior was totally unacceptable for a Day. I didn't think I would hear the end of that. In football, if I was hit inappropriately and felt the need to square that away on the next play, that behavior was considered beneath a Day. All of those things added up in my mind about the correct way to play the game of life. The events from being married to buying a first home to receiving a second degree were just as important to the entire family as they were to me and my brothers personally. At the age of twenty-seven, when I received a Masters of Science in Administration with concentration in Computer Science from George Washington University, one might have thought I was just awarded a Ph.D. from Harvard. Our parents focused on our success with such crucial components as the celebration of accomplishments, the coaching and the counseling, the expression of genuine feelings about getting a job, receiving an award, getting a promotion, or receiving a raise. And they did it without making a big deal out of it to others!

To make ends meet, it was necessary to have a boarding house. Part of the guidance we received was to stay away from wrong elements, even if on occasion those elements managed to live next door. This lesson was an important aspect of raising boys who might easily have explored many negative options and neighborhood temptations. After all, we were only two blocks from the "bed and breakfast" referred to as Susie and Jimmy's, at 37th and West Broad. That was the type of place that was known to rent the same room multiple times in a 24-hour period. Drugs and crime were common, though in milder form in the '50s and '60s than is now the case.

Right after earning a masters degree, I was interviewed for five or six positions with top companies in the United States. Industries included oil, pharmaceuticals, insurance, banking, chemical, transportation, and the like. I decided to leave the East Coast, newly married, with pressures of settling down to start a family, to join a nationally based airline at its computer center in Denver, Colorado. This may have been a temporary heartbreak for my parents, who were happy to see me married before thirty and settling down, but sad that I would live so far away. Many families from Savannah, including my parents, were not accustomed to the idea of changing jobs let alone changing cities on a whim.

However, with my generation in the early 70's, different jobs two or three times before settling was expected in order to get a $2,500 or $5,000 per year increase in salary. I also could not resist the adventure of moving to a distant city and the flying benefits to foreign lands that came with working for an airline. This was an opportunity to see the world–especially when that option was not possible through the military.

Continuing to stay in a city such as Washington, D.C., within fifty minutes of waters to fish, would have given me an opportunity to establish a possible retirement location alternative for my parents. A year earlier, I'd had the chance to take Daddy on a terrific fishing trip on a chartered boat on Chesapeake Bay. I would have loved to do more of that. But I yearned to move on.

There was emphasis on children's success and for us to have it a little better with less pain and difficulty. My parents feared the difficulty that comes from having a tough job. Our success seemed to be a real goal for them and I believe for Daddy in particular. In other words, having a job that you really like can be rare. Daddy never complained about his job directly to us, about how hard he had to work, how frustrating it must have been. On one occasion I spoke with my brother about the potential of speaking to Police Superintendent Barnes to ask why Daddy hadn't been promoted. My brother quickly replied "Daddy would have killed you." I realized that those frustrations of not being promoted but nevertheless living a life that he felt made a difference for others without expecting payback was a powerful statement of our father's character. This was the work ethic he lived. This drive formed my determination to always make things work and, while I'm at it, to help other people. It really is the true essence of being spiritually driven. This still guides me today.

Daddy demonstrated this focus on others in mentoring younger officers. It is probably an outgrowth of his beliefs about himself and in others. He set the stage for others to not only follow, but to lead and excel technically in the field of criminal justice.

It is clear that our well being was more important. Our parents' personal goals showed their priorities were their children's education, training and confidence to make it further! Our every accomplishment became personally important to them and our success in many ways became theirs, too. Mama's and Daddy's motives and attention came from their desire to see our potential realized. Our successes were credited to our efforts, not theirs, supported by encouragement and praise. There was never ever a push for excellence or to succeed for the sake of being better than anyone else, but rather to be all that we could be, utilizing every gift and skill we could muster for our own personal gain. We also learned from their example that helping someone else achieve success along the way is also quite rewarding and in fact is a measure of success in and of itself.

The Bridge Builder

An old man going a lone highway

Came in the evening at the close of day

To a chasm vast, deep and wide

The old man crossed in the twilight dim

The sullen stream had no fear for him

But he paused when safe on the other side

And built a bridge that would span the tide

Old man, said a fellow traveler near

You're wasting your time by building here

Your journey will end at the close of day

You'll never again pass this way

You've crossed the chasm vast and wide

Why build you this bridge at evening tide

The old man lifted his old gray head

My friend in the way I've come, he said,

There follows after me today

A youth whose feet must pass this way

This stream which has been as naught to me

To the fair haired youth might a pitfall be

He too must cross in the twilight dim

Good friend, I'm building this bridge for him

Will Allen Dromgoole   1860-1934

Chapter 16
The Last Full Measure of Devotion

In 1972, Robert was seventeen and the only son remaining at home. He saw first hand Daddy's continuing struggles and the strain of all the pressures of maintaining the income to ensure private school and college for his youngest and security for his wife. The short-term rental of rooms and apartments supplemented his salary, but the maintenance and problems associated with owning the property also added to the stress. Daddy's salary did not increase with seniority and never exceeded $12,000. From 1947 to 1972 Daddy served his entire twenty-five year career as a Private, First Class Officer. His two oldest sons had surpassed his income and received promotions and advancement opportunities within three years of their college graduation. While this was a source of deep pride, it must have also been a wake-up call to the realization of how much he had given in service in a difficult work environment with such little financial return.

The pressures of this life manifested themselves in many different ways. The chores that once were shared by two older brothers were now resting solely on the shoulders of the youngest son to help Daddy get ready for work, polish the brass, the Savannah Police Department collar pins (SPDs), police badge, buckles and those extremely heavy black walking shoes. On some occasions, cleaning all of the leather belts, handcuffs case, and metal emblem on the police cap was also part of the chores. Daddy, however, always cleaned his own gun.

After many years policing the streets and neighborhoods in a relatively small town, he avoided the stress of off-duty public situations where those whom he had arrested for some misdemeanor might challenge him. An example is a trip with Robert and Mama to Darien, Georgia, outside of Brunswick, to an amusement park with a small water hole the family used to frequent during the early years. On this occasion, Daddy was approached by two men wanting to even the score from some prior police action. The two men, who had been drinking, began to talk "trash" and brought their razzing close up into Daddy's face. Daddy took a step back, back handed one with the power and swing of a man half his age, knocking him to the ground. At almost the same time, he had his revolver drawn on the other. The two men quickly backed off. Of course, the men were testing and might have felt they could beat up a police officer and get away with it. The bigger implication was this constant threat that anyone, at any time, might succeed in causing injury or even death. This time it spoiled yet another outing for Robert and Mama and they left immediately to avoid any further incident. Such became the way of life as years went on.

As Daddy became more homebound to avoid the potential for ruckus in the public, a pattern emerged of expecting others to retrieve the television remote, bring water or juice or to otherwise take care of things. His health and weight may have also contributed to reduced physical effort when he was home and off duty. One of the results of the sedentary lifestyle may have been his first heart attack at age 55.

I don't know if that helped my mother with what was to come. She did seem to be prepared for Daddy's death in a way that was unusual. As a police officer, he was always on guard, always suspicious, looking for something that wasn't right. This wears a family down. And there was also the professional secrecy. Daddy couldn't talk about people he arrested or describe how his day went, like other husbands could. Police officers had a high divorce rate, and some were known to beat their spouses. Although that never happened in our house, I could feel it when there was high tension—which was fairly often.

In the late 1960s and early '70s, after the parks were integrated, Daddy was assigned to walk Forsyth Park. Basketball, football, tennis and other games attracted large crowds and east-west wars between teenagers. Twenty years of changes in Savannah during many years of police work meant a change from watching older sons play basketball and football as a parent enjoying the game to watching out for the safety and security of the remaining son.

The combination of pressures from a job where confrontation, death or injury were routine, the frustration of making ends meet, and the reality of being a homeowner and property manager with mostly unstable week-to-week wage earners took a toll on Daddy and our family. Skirmishes at home had the effect of hardening personalities just enough to prepare remaining family members for life going forward without Daddy. This is an odd concept, that the small deeds and the ways of everyday living crystallized as a protective shield, bringing the realization that one day we will all be left alone. Mama and Robert must have felt this process happening and understood it without compromising their love and understanding Daddy's situation. There were trying moments of taking the talk, bossing around and ordering the to-dos.

It was early morning, Saturday, April 1, 1972. After working his shift, Daddy had arrived at home and had stretched across his bed still in uniform, too exhausted to undress. He had worked the 3:00 p.m. to 11:00 p.m. shift the night before. It was not uncommon for him to spend an additional two hours, especially on a Friday night, to finish up paperwork and make the drive from East Oglethorpe to Burroughs Street.

David Jones, a former Savannah policeman and an officer during the latter years of Daddy's career remembered events in the months leading to that morning. He recalled that three months earlier Daddy had been assigned to work the paddy wagon, which is considerably less stressful than driving a patrol car or walking a beat even on a limited area assignment such as Forsyth Park. Of course no one knows the reason for the abrupt reassignment to walking a beat again. Perhaps Daddy had raised a question or pointed out an issue to management as he had been known to do. Fridays and Saturdays are the most demanding days and evenings of a police week. That Friday night was no exception. Friday night at the end of the month and the workweek was payday for many and the beginning of a long weekend with rough crowds.

While on patrol duty, during what appeared to be a routine arrest, a suspect turned on the police, Daddy in particular. This scuffle added to the stress for the 6 foot, 240 pound man with a heart condition.

Robert worked at the Pirate's House Restaurant across town and was just getting home around 1:00 a.m. Saturday morning. As he entered the house, he heard a loud boom that sounded to him like a big cannon or a gun. In retrospect, it set the stage in his mind that something significant was about to happen. It was not uncommon for a ruckus to break out, even though renters knew their landlord was a policeman. Robert could not see anything and could not identify the source of the noise except that it seemed to come from upstairs where there were two rental units. He rushed to wake Daddy, whom he found fully clothed in uniform and shoes, to come and investigate, leaving Mama asleep. Considering the day of the week, time of the morning, and the type of noise meant probable big trouble, Daddy immediately picked up his 38 police special revolver and ensured it was fully loaded. He told Robert to get his own gun, meaning Robert's 22 caliber rifle with which he was trained as a marksman. As both son and Daddy went to the porch, all seemed strangely quiet.

Daddy instructed Robert to remain on the porch while he went up to Unit 2208 first. He said that if anyone came out of the door before he returned, Robert should shoot. After three to four minutes of checking, all seemed to be clear. Daddy indicated as much and returned to the porch where

Robert stood ready. Next, he went to check Unit 2206. Still the night remained silent, with no signs that anyone else was even curious. Daddy proceeded upstairs checking for trouble or the origin of the loud, booming noise. Again, Robert was instructed to shoot if Daddy wasn't the first one out. All was in place with no intruders in the second unit as well, and Daddy returned to the porch. The lower level, 2204, was not checked because Robert was certain that the noise came from above.

In case an intruder might be lying low after creating the ruckus, Daddy told Robert to go on in and prepare for bed, while he remained on the porch to check things out further. It was not more than three minutes after Robert had gone inside and headed to his room that he heard a loud, panicked shout from his father, "Robert, Robert, come quickly". It was not a usual sound because it was very seldom that any of the family members had ever heard panic in our father's voice. Robert hustled to get to the porch to find Daddy staggering, reaching for the rail and nearly falling down the concrete steps. It was clear that Daddy was not shot or hurt by an intruder but was having excruciating pains from within. Trying to sit down on the top step, Daddy was falling forward down the steps when Robert slid himself underneath to break his fall. Daddy's facial expression expressed pain and fear, he was excessively pale, and his fists were as tight as rocks. Robert was by now holding the full weight of his Daddy and screamed for his mother, "Mama, Mama." It took several shouts for Mama to awaken and come to the front to see what was wrong. She quickly realized that an ambulance was needed and rushed to call 911 for help. When she returned to the porch, she took her husband in her arms, relieving Robert. The ambulance arrived quickly, within five minutes, but it appeared to be too late. Daddy had had a massive heart attack. He was 59.

The EMS team said very little and proceeded to take Daddy to Memorial Hospital. Mama did not ride in the ambulance but called Fess. She must have realized Daddy's stillness was a clear sign of death. Under normal circumstances, the nitroglycerin tablets, which he carried in a small container in his pocket, would have sufficed to help him through the moment. But the massive, painful and sudden heart attack occurred too quickly. For Daddy, and for Robert, too, it must have seemed an eternity of suffering. Rev. Oliver arrived quickly to take Mama to the hospital, leaving Robert to call family members before following in Daddy's car.

Hospitals were still strict and wouldn't tell Robert what had occurred. But once he'd learned his mother had just left, he realized his Daddy had died. He wondered if he'd done all that he could have done in prolonging Daddy's life. In the eyes of his brothers and family, he responded as well as anyone could have in such a traumatic crisis and he protected Daddy as best he could to the very end.

In the days after his death, there were those in Savannah who explained the loud boom that Robert heard that night to be symbolic of something traumatic and urgent about to happen. In other words, the boom was a sign, a stage setting, a preparatory noise to alert the young son of what was about to happen so he would remember every detail leading up to and about the death of his father.

Voodoo and casting of spells was commonly talked about in the southeastern United States, and Savannah was no exception. People were very big on that in the South. They would perform ceremonies, almost like a prayerful procession, to cause harm to someone else and have them suffer because of some misdeed they had done to them or someone else. There are those who would have you believe that because of Daddy's police work, arrests—and, in particular, his shooting and killing of a civilian during the civil rights movement—that such a spell had been cast on the aging police officer.

Thinking back to the final months of life for Daddy, it is easy to reflect on the preparation in relation to the family for what was about to happen. It is noticeable how the attitudes and day-to-day communication changed within our family as the aging patriarch, sometimes larger-than-life father, began to decline in vigor.

Reflectively, we all seem to deal with a life built over time with fortification relative to those we love deeply. Mama, my brothers and I all adjusted to Daddy's change in behavior and attitudes in our own ways. We recognized that Daddy's experiences, most of which we never knew, and his acceptance of immovable barriers to his career development affected him and resulted in enormous stress. This happened gradually over a long period as we all came to recognize the high price he paid to provide for us and how deeply we loved him.

The last days and hours of life for Daddy must have been among the most traumatic of his entire career. The events leading up to his final breath and manner in which he died leave us all with deep regrets that things had not worked out differently. His life was shortened by the struggles of living, working and being himself. Yet there is that peace and comfort in knowing that he would have done it all over again, close to the same way! We wish he could see the results of his efforts and what's happened since his early death.

Robert remembers Daddy differently than do Bill and I. By then our brother, Edmund, the third son had passed away. Patsy, our half sister, had moved on to New York City and had lost contact with most of the family. Daddy, at 59 years of age, weighed approximately 240 pounds and stood 6 feet tall. While he had stopped drinking beer and even given up cigars at this point in his life, the stress of police work and the potential for struggling with men and women much younger and in better shape was always present in a day's work. Also, the anxieties of politics in the workplace are no different in police business than any other work environment.

William Day, Sr. lived his life with determination, pride, courage, and integrity. He touched many lives along the way and made full use of his intelligence and experience to guide and support his family and his community. He lived in the face of prejudice and danger every day as a police officer. Those who loved him paid a price with him, feeling his stress and his distress, even when he was off duty. Our family held together through love and caring and we knew that our relationships with one another were our strength.

That strength sustained Mama after Daddy's death and has served me and my brothers well. The lives they created, nurtured, and supported to become independent, productive adults, loving parents, and adoring grandparents. Daddy's legacy lives on in the scores of family members who continue to embody his lessons of responsibility and success. Thank you, Daddy. Thank you, Mama. Thank you, Officer Day.

EPILOGUE

Selected Headlines from the *Savannah Tribune*

November 1946
$500.00 Reward for Information on the Killing of a Policeman
(Miami)

January 1947
Talmadge Wins Governorship, Arnall Refusing to Relinquish
Office
Cops Jail Couple for Having New Car in Louisiana

February 1947
South Carolina Mob Stages First Lynching of the Year

May 1947
Savannah Gets Her First Negro Policemen
Squad of Nine Presented to Public at Center Dedication

May 1947
Day Succeeds Grant as City Policeman

July 1947
Nine Negro Police Officers Appointed Last May
First in Parade, Led by Officer Milton Hall

July 1947
Picture Scenes from Police Banquet Waldburg and Burroughs

December 1947

City to Appoint Three More Negro Policemen

February 1949

Two Negro Policemen Dismissed from Force; and the Current
Shake-Up in the Police Department . . . Lercy Wilson and Milton
Hall

August 1955

Board of Education Hurls Ultimatum at Teachers. Says They Must
Quit the NAACP by September 15th or Lose Their Jobs
W.W. Law, President of Savannah branch of NAACP

September 1955

Police Department Appoints Five Negro Women School Traffic
Officers

December 1955

Another Civic Leader NAACP Worker Shot in His Store in
Mississippi
Woman Fined for Refusing to Vacate Her Seat in White Section of
Bus

January 1956

Jim Crow Public Housing Banned in St. Louis
White/Colored Signs Removed at Union Station
Catholic Bishop Says Segregation Cannot Endure Too Long
Local NAACP Branch to Open Membership Drive Sunday

March 1956 Editorial

More Policemen. It has been a disappointment that only 10 or 11 Negro officers have been employed and that their activity has been so restricted.

August 1956

Dr. Ralph Mark Gilbert's Funeral

March 1958

Martin Luther King, Jr. is in New York Hospital Suffering from Complications of Pneumonia Following Unexplained Stabbing

July 1958

The Rev. Martin Luther King, Jr. Writes Moving Account of Montgomery Bus Boycott and "Stride Toward Freedom"

August 1958

Court Refuses to Delay Integration (Little Rock)

Local NAACP to Protest Acquittal of Officer Who Shot 13-Year-Old Boy

September 1958

The Rev. Martin Luther King, Jr. Arrested in Montgomery, Alabama

School Integration, Pro and Con

The Rev. Martin Luther King Has Fair Chance to Recover From Stabbing by Woman

November 1958 Editorial

Deservedly Commended Praise of Police Department; 16 Negro
Policemen under Chief Sydney B. Barnes

January 1959 Editorial

Negro Policemen Needed

March 1959

Student Boycott Results in School Bus Transportation Johnson
High School

December 1959

Citizens Betterment Association to Sponsor Campaign for 20,000
Registered Voters in Chatham County

February 1960

Lunch Counter Sit-Downs Encompass 11 Cities
Dr. King Charges Persecution in Indictment for Income Tax
Evasion

March 1960

Local Lunch Counter Sit-Downs Continue
Levy's Sit-Down Demonstration Began Last Week

April 1960

Mayor's Bi-Racial Committee Denounced by NAACP

May 1960

Anti-Picketing Law Passed by City Council
Sit-Downers Sentenced

July 1960
250 Robed KKK March Down Broughton Street

August 6, 1960
Youthful Kneel-Ins Welcome at Two White Churches, Five
Churches Refuse to Admit Them

Selected Headlines from the *Savannah Herald*

October 1950
Segregation is Discrimination – NAACP

May 1958
Eleven Years with Savannah's Finest

March 1960
NAACP Backs Sit-Ins at Mass Meeting

April 1960
NAACP Slaps Easter Bunny at Mass Meeting, Agreed to Withhold
All Easter Purchases from Downtown Stores
The Savannah Scene Has Become of National Note; The Local Sit-
In Situation Has Spread the City's Name
2,000 Attend 6th NAACP Mass Meeting; Youngsters Who Were
Arrested Last Week While Participating in Sit-In and Those Who
Were Arrested While Walking Through Forsyth Park

July 1960

Ezell Blair, 16th NAACP Mass Meeting Speaker, Sunday

NAACP Youth Leader Stirs 17th Mass Meeting

NAACP Stages Mammoth March on Eve of Democratic Meeting

September 1960

Crusade for Voters Sparks High Negro Voting in Primary

October 1960

Mercedes Wright 29th Mass Meeting Speaker Calls for Continuous Broughton Street Boycott

November 1960

WW Law Reelected State NAACP Head

July 1961

Savannah Lunch Counters to Integrate

Negroes Back Boycott Lift

September 1961

Citizens Write Up a Letter Concerning Law Dismissal

September 1965

NAACP Mass Meeting at First Mt. Sinai

Open Letter to Father Toomey Concerning W.W. Law

October 1965

NAACP Roundup of Special Projects

Carolyn Quilloin was in group arrested in 1960 which started the local NAACP Freedom Now Movement.

February 6, 1968
W.W. Law Turned Away from White Methodist Church

March 1968
Chatham Crusade for Voters to Hear Dr. Martin Luther King, Jr.

April 1968
Large Crowd Attends NAACP Rites for Dr. King
Editorial – The Route of Riots by Sidney A. Jones

September 1971
Patrolling the Main Stem

April 1972
Officer William J. Day, Sr. passed away Saturday, April 1, 1972, after working his shift at the Savannah Police Department and arriving home.

APPENDIX

The City of Savannah

The following discussions on major landmarks, industries, waterways and islands, military bases and readiness, architecture, churches, schools and universities will provide a backdrop of where the Day family and other Savannahians lived and worked. Savannah today is known just as much for its tourism as it is for being a major seaport; and certainly more so than being the agricultural center that brought the city into being. There are also several major landmarks that distinguish this city of beauty and charm.

Major Landmarks

Savannah's downtown district became an historical landmark as of 1966. Despite devastating fires in 1796 and 1820, many of the 18th and 19th century homes have been restored. Some twenty-four squares are included in and around the historic district. River Street near Factor's Walk stands out as one of the most frequently visited areas in Savannah. Located on the waterfront, its cobblestone drive and winding streets provide access to and from the city's riverside. River Street and Bay Street are also near Savannah's City Hall. A new Civic Center that opened in Savannah about 1971 is located on Orion Square, the site of the 1917 City Auditorium. The river area hosted boating events for the 1996 Olympic Games, which were centered in Atlanta.

Savannah has become known nationwide for its St. Patrick's Day Parade—one of the largest St. Patrick's Day celebrations in the country. More than 300,000 visitors fill the city for this event. Savannah has also hosted a number of U.S. presidents during their time in office. In 1962, former President Harry Truman visited Savannah during the annual St. Patrick's Day Parade and festivities and addressed the Hibernian Society's annual banquet.

In 1962, President John F. Kennedy paid tribute to military personnel at Ft. Stewart's Army Base in nearby Liberty County. Lyndon Baines Johnson arrived in 1964 to survey damage in nearby Brunswick following Hurricane Dora, The area was declared a disaster site qualifying for Federal aid. And of course there was Georgia's own state governor, Jimmy Carter, who visited in 1974 where he spoke at the Savannah News-Press building on Bay Street.

In addition to popular landmarks, Savannah has made its reputation with various industries, its unique oceanfront location with waterways and islands, and its prominence in supporting war and other national defense measures with military readiness. Savannah has also maintained its charm, with architecture in the historic district, and is well known for many of its churches. Finally, a number of schools, colleges, and universities have evolved as city institutions. Many have open campus environments where sprawling pine, oak trees and Spanish moss abound.

Industries

Through the years Savannah has transitioned to the industries of agriculture, manufacturing and seaport operations. Here is a sample of some of the more influential businesses that contributed significantly to distinguish Savannah's commerce and productivity.

Union Bag Corporation

Union Camp Corporation, formerly Union Bag, employs nearly 400 Savannahians in a huge and distinctive manufacturing operation on more than 400 acres beside the Savannah River. The plant's operation involves pulp and paper, a corrugated box factory, a paper plant, and a chemical manufacturing plant. The economic impact of Union Camp's operation is estimated at more than one-half billion dollars annually.

The Georgia Ports Authority

The Georgia Ports Authority, established in 1945, operates with a 220-acre ocean terminal in downtown Savannah plus nearby Garden City's 856-acre terminal, where collectively more than six million tons of cargo is handled each year. Since the majority of world goods are shipped via container, the container port facility in Savannah actively handles more than three million tons of containerized cargo annually. Statewide, the economic impact of the Georgia Ports Authority is responsible for more than 58,000 jobs—roughly under $200 million in state and local taxes and customs operations, which nets annually more than $200 million at the Port of Savannah.

Savannah Foods & Industries, Inc.

Savannah Foods & Industries, Inc., formerly the Savannah Sugar Refinery, incorporated in 1916, has been the second largest sugar refinery in the country. In 1997, Savannah Foods acquired Imperial Sugar Company, thus becoming the largest processor and refinery of sugar in the U.S. In the mid 1800s, farmers produced sugar by using horse powered mills to grind local sugar cane after cooking the cane juice in an open air boiling pan. Savannah Foods & Industries, Inc. now refines both beet and sugar cane for sale in a variety of forms to consumers and processors. Brand names include Dixie Crystal, Evercane, Savannah Gold, Sweet Things and Pioneer. The company also packages and distributes other products, such as custom meal kits, salt and pepper, artificial sweetener, non-dairy creamer, and other products that complement the sugar business.

GulfStream Aerospace Corporation

Grumman Aircraft Company was founded in 1958. In 1978, Allen E. Paulson purchased the company and changed the name to Gulf Stream Aerospace Corporation, which specialized in building high-performance corporate jets. GulfStream is a wholly-owned subsidiary of General Dynamics Corporation. The company has built more than 14,000 aircraft for corporate, government, private and military customers around the world. GulfStream has facilities in Appleton, Wisconsin; Brunswick, New Jersey; Dallas, Texas and Long Beach, California. Savannah is where state-of-the-art technology is used for manufacturing high-speed jets. There are some 3,500 men and women at GulfStream in Savannah. It is one of Chatham County's largest employers with nearly two million square feet of corporate offices and manufacturing facility near the Savannah International Airport. Bill Cosby, an owner of a GulfStream jet, was said to have visited Savannah during routine service and maintenance of his aircraft.

The Great Dane Trailers Company

A company by the name of Savannah Blowpipe Company was established in 1900 in Savannah with a total capitalization of $3,000. The company's core business at that time tended toward dust and chip correcting systems for sawmills and furniture plants throughout the southeast.

In 1931, the company was incorporated as the Steel Products Company, with assets of approximately $100,000. With a company vision, which included seizing the opportunity inherent for the development for better highways in the southeast, the management decided to manufacture truck trailers for over-the-road freight hauling. The company's Greenville, South Carolina facility was the source of the Great Dane name as well as expertise for trailer manufacturing. Great Dane pioneered the refrigerated trailer and built the first produce van with a wet ice bunker and motor and lower cooler systems. Refrigerated vans soon followed. Since 1953, the refrigerated aluminum trailers have been in much demand throughout the southeast, especially with the Florida perishables market, which enabled the company to exceed $6 million annually and establish sales outlets in 31 cities and 18 states across the eastern half of the U.S. In 1972 Great Dane acquired Arrow Trailers Company of Memphis, Texas, where platform trailers are also constructed. In 1977 the Great Dane Company merged with Pines Trailers, creating the Great Dane Limited Partnership, the world's largest trailer company. Both companies began as family-owned operations and the merged companies' top management is still involved with diverse business lines and operations. As an interesting note, the Great Dane Company owns and operates the Grove Point Plantation, which was built in 1886 and located on property originally developed on a land grant from King George III. It is used as an executive guest house and hunting lodge.

Tourism

Tourism has become one of Savannah's largest industries, with significant influence on the local economy, including employment and retail sales. In 2002 travel expenditures in Savannah exceeded $1 billion. The U.S. Department of Labor estimates that some 15,000 jobs were supported by tourism in 2002 with growth in travel-related dining, retail, food services, transportation, entertainment and recreation. The Savannah Music and Film Festivals, the St. Patrick's Day celebration, offshore power boat racing—which alone accounted for 75,000 visitors in July 2002—as well as the inauguration of the Liberty Mutual Legends of Golf event are all credited with contributing to Savannah's tourism growth.

Waterways and Islands

There are some sixteen islands and waterways that border Savannah and the Chatham County area. Some of the most notable islands include Wilmington, Skidaway, Tybee, Wassaw, Dutch/Liberty, and Ossabaw. Several of these islands and a few others in the broader coastal area constitute the Barrier Island, which includes Tybee, Wassaw, Ossabaw, St. Catherine's, Light Beard, Sapelo,

St. Simon's, Jekyll, White Marsh Island, and Cumberland. Over the years, the islands have been used as landing points, agricultural centers, water sports arenas, family dwellings, resorts, military preparedness and wildlife refuge and sanctuaries. Salt marshes and tidal creeks close in and about the 16 islands and interconnecting rivers and waterways.

Wilmington Island, some 8,000 acres in size, is easily accessed from the Thunderbolt area in Savannah and houses a number of homes, yachts, country clubs, marinas, and launch pads for fishing boats. The parade of fishing boats in the early morning from Thunderbolt near the Thunderbolt Bridge and around Wilmington Island seaward is an awesome sight and is of great commercial importance as well as a pleasure for onlookers.

White Marsh Island is approximately twelve miles southeast of Savannah and is bound by the Wilmington River on the west and south, Richardson Creek on the north, and Turner's Creek on the east. This island was a settlement for Native Americans as well as European colonists who built homes and lived on the island with their families.

Turner's Lock, once known as Lacy's Island, is less than 200 acres in size and located on the southeast sector near White Marsh Island. It is bordered by Bradley Creek on the east, Turner's Creek on the north and east, and the

Wilmington River, which was called the Skidaway River in colonial times.

Skidaway Island, some eight to ten miles south of Savannah, is less than nine miles long and three miles wide. Because of its proximity to Savannah, it served over the years as a lookout point as well as an area for agriculture, especially cotton.

Tybee Island is located near the mouth of the Savannah River and serves as a barrier island in the northern most part of Chatham County. Its location, as is true of the Cocksbur and Little Tybee Islands, has been of military importance throughout history. Spain, France and England, along with the U.S. colonies all claimed ownership at one time. These islands were inhabited initially by Native Americans, who took great interest in their natural resources, including sassafras. Elizabeth Carpenter Piechocinski's book *Once Upon an Island* is a litany of family ownership, naming conventions, military history, home ownership and the impact of hurricanes as well as some history of Negro slaves and island plantation owners.

A very practical island for Savannahians to visit by way of the Savannah River was Defuskie Island in South Carolina. Trips to Defuskie during summer months involve boat rides and seafood and still are a major attraction for many. This island, linked by bridges, seems almost as an extension of the city proper.

Marshes in the Savannah area are believed to be the richest acreage on earth. Savannah stands out as having more than 700,000 acres of salt marshes, swamps, and mud flats.

It would be remiss to not remember the Ogeechee River. Much is said about Savannah's marsh land; there are a lot of swampy woods for fisherman and hunters alike. While the river has reddish, blue-green, and blackish tones before it meets the ocean, there are areas along the riverbank that still provide great fun and excitement for fishermen who love catching Ogeechee chad or a prize catfish.

Military History and Modern Day Readiness

Military installations in and around Savannah have historical relevance for city tourism and active combat importance, most recently as part of Operation Iraqi Freedom. Hunter Army Airfield and Ft. Steward provide well over 40,000 jobs between them, half of which are civilian and the other military. These contribute some $2 billion annually to Savannah's economy. In addition to Ft. Steward, the Marine Corps Air Station in Beauford, SC, the Naval Hospital of Beauford, Hunter Army Airfield, the U.S. Coast Guard, and the Navy's Submarine Base all contribute to the Iraq war effort. Apache and Blackhawk helicopters, along with C130 flight and support crews and F18 flight and support crews, are all among military services located in the Savannah area. More than 20,000 troops plus mobilized National Guard and reserve troops have been processed and deployed for Iraq through the Ft. Steward/Hunter Airfield complex.

Savannah is also home to the Air Guard's Combat Readiness Training Center, a unique facility operating critical offshore bombing ranges used by all branches of the military. These same military facilities in the Savannah area were instrumental in the Desert Storm initiative as well.

The importance of Savannah's militarily strategic location dates back long before Desert Storm and Operation Iraqi Freedom. Ft. Pulaski was the site of a defining event that occurred during the American Civil War. In April 1864, Union troops directed rifle and cannon fire at the fort and breached the southeast angle. The capability and accuracy of this rifle cannon made brick fortifications obsolete.

During this time frame, Union Major General David Hunter, an abolitionist, ordered the release of area slaves and many were then recruited into the Union army. This became the first South Carolina Colored Regiment.

Ft. Pulaski Park was named as a tourist attraction with scenic marsh and variety of animal life, in a combination with palm and pine trees where a variety of wetland grasses abound. Another fort on Tybee Island—Ft. Screven—played a key role in the war against Spain over the treatment of the people of Cuba during William McKinley's administration. Ft. Screven was constructed to guard the entrances to Savannah and other nearby cities such as Brunswick, St. Mary's and Darien. From 1897 to 1947, Ft. Screven was a valuable part of America's coastal defense system. Troops trained and maintained guard on Tybee Island through the Spanish American War of 1898, World War I and WW II. In 1947 the fort was closed and sold to the town of Tybee.

Ft. Jackson, the sole standing brick fortification in Georgia, was constructed in 1808 and replaced a fort built earlier called Mud Fort. The fort's name was taken from James Jackson, Governor of Georgia and a Revolutionary War colonel. Ft. Jackson served as the headquarters for the Confederate defense, defenses of the Savannah River during the Civil War. The Coastal Heritage Society maintains this site as well as the Savannah History Museum, a railroad history museum for the state, and the CSS Georgia, sunk in the Savannah River in December 1864.

Architecture

Gen. James Oglethorpe's plan for the city of Savannah was created by an English architect, William Jay, in 1817. The Land Regency style of architecture began in the city of Savannah, and several of the original homes built in 1700 to 1850 that remain preserved in the city have become tourist attractions. The original homes and buildings were sturdy, symmetrical and built with stone, brick and wood. Servants' quarters and carriage houses were typically placed at the rear of the lot, accessible to a rear alley. The Richardson-Owens-Toddler House, run by the Telfair Academy of Arts and Sciences, is an example of William Jay's architectural work. The Telfair Academy Museum building is the Alexander Telfair House, which served as the Governor of Georgia's residence in the mid 1700s.

The William-Scarbrough House is another example of an original home in Savannah, where President James Monroe visited and slept. New Yorker John S. Norris introduced a gothic revival style in the city. The Green-Meldrim House would serve as headquarters for General Sherman during the Civil War. The residence is now the parish house for St. John's Episcopal Church. Savannah's historic district, approximately three square miles in area, embodies more than 2,000 historically and architecturally significant buildings. There is also a Victorian District where houses have a "gingerbread trim."

Savannah is also known for magnificent squares in the downtown area. An important component of the Oglethorpe plan, some twenty-four squares have been refurbished and serve as garden areas, monuments, memorial centers, and park settings with benches. These squares are typically lined with live oak and magnolia trees with Spanish moss draping the tree branches. Plants such as azaleas contribute decorative color. Savannah is also blessed with large parks such as the Forsyth Park, which was developed in 1851. It still remains a center with sporting activities, flower watching and gardens of tourist interest. Forsyth Park was referenced in the book and movie, *Midnight in the Garden of Good and Evil*, where the man walked an invisible dog with a leash in order to fulfill his requirement for services provided after the owner's death.

Laurel Grove and Bonaventure Cemeteries are historic sites of their own and are lined with trees and plants indigenous to Savannah. These trees and plants, many flowering in season, add to the beauty of these two historic cemeteries. Perhaps the most stunning view of azaleas can be seen in season on a "17-mile drive" from Savannah City to Tybee Beach area on Victory Drive. Palm trees also line the street, which was named for Sherman's march to sea during the capture of Savannah. Azaleas and palm trees lace Victory Drive most of the distance from downtown to the Tybee beach area.

Churches

While many of the Savannah historic buildings survived on their own, a number have been restored. The restored churches in Savannah include the Lutheran Church of Ascension, dating back to 1741; the First African Baptist Church, and the First Bryan Baptist Church, both dating back to 1788; the Cathedral of St. John the Baptist, 1876; the Independent Presbyterian Church of 1890; St. Stephen's Episcopal (Unitarian) Church, 1855; the Temple Mickevee Israel, founded in 1733, the third oldest synagogue in America; and St. Phillips Monumental AME, Georgia's oldest African Methodist Episcopal Congregation, which was founded in 1865.

Schools, Colleges and Universities

Savannah State University, located at Savannah's marsh waterfront in Thunderbolt, is the oldest public historically black college in Georgia. Founded in 1890 as a state land grant institution, the university has approximately 3,000 students and just less than 200 acres of land or buildings spread-out in a true campus environment. The university offers both graduate and undergraduate degrees in business administration, liberal arts, social sciences, and science and technology. The university excels in marine sciences. SSU was originally named The Georgia State Industrial College for Colored Youth. A degree program was instituted in 1928, and in 1937 the college was renamed Georgia State College. It became the Savannah State College in 1950, and in 1996 its name was changed to Savannah State University.

Armstrong Atlantic State University was founded in 1935 as Armstrong Junior College and became a campus of the university system of Georgia and a two-year program in 1959. In 1996 Armstrong became a four-year institution and the name was changed to Armstrong Atlantic State University. Originally an historic district college across from Forsyth Park, Armstrong Atlantic State University has relocated south of downtown on a 250-acre urban campus with some 5,500 full- and part-time students. AASU offers about sixty-four undergraduate and eleven graduate degree programs in arts and sciences, teacher education, and the health professions. The institution also serves as the regional health professional center and a regional criminal justice training center. It recently became part of the Georgia Tech regional engineering program. The institution has also become part of the Yamacraw Mission, a group of eight state universities offering highly specialized curricula in order to attract high-tech companies to Georgia.

The Savannah College of Art and Design (SCAD) was founded in 1978 to provide a degree program as a specialized professional art college. The school has grown tremendously since 1979 and has purchased numerous properties around Savannah as classroom buildings, studios, galleries, computer labs, film and television editing suites, darkrooms, residential halls, and offices. Recently SCAD has added a book store, two diners, a tearoom, several theaters, facilities for fine arts, performing arts, industrial design fabrication, and film and video processing as well as two fitness centers and an 85,000-square-foot library.

Currently, SCAD has more than fifty facilities and offers a bachelor of fine arts, masters of arts and architecture, and twenty plus majors from animation to graphic design, interior design and visual effects and media and performing arts. Six thousand students from all 50 states and more than 80 countries attend SCAD's degreed programs. Ten percent of the student body is from abroad.

On balance, Savannah has fared well and remains a southern city proud of its heritage, significance in world events and contribution to the nation in its growth, development and in dealing with civil strife. More importantly, it has served as home for many families who have witnessed the changes over time and endured by caring for its own, remaining open and hospitable to visitors, and offering a cultural and proud history for all to see first hand!

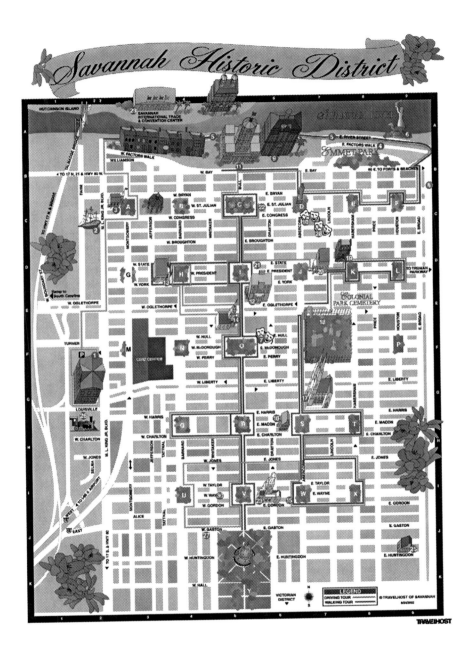

191

CHARLES E. DAY, CMC, FIMC

A native of Savannah, GA, former airline executive and founder of Charles E. Day and Associates LLC in Alexandria, VA, Charles E. Day Sr. is author of a McGraw-Hill book, *Call Center Operations: Profiting From Teleservices*; co-author of *Best Practices for a Continually Improving Customer Responsive Organization*; and contributor to the *Handbook of Management Consulting Services*. His management consulting firm specializes in the areas of customer service, business process reviews, and technology transfer.

After 35 years of marriage, Charles E. Day Sr. is the father of two sons and has two granddaughters and a grandson who live in the Washington, DC, area. At St.

John's Episcopal Church in Fort Washington, MD, he serves as a Lay Eucharist Minister and sings in the choir. He is co-founder and sings with the Fort Washington Community Chorus. Charles sings with the Metropolitan Chorus in Washington, DC and has held several leadership positions. Charles has acted in two productions of the Tantallon Community Players in Fort Washington, MD, portraying Booker T. Washington in their adaptation of the Broadway musical *Ragtime* and the Reverend Sykes in the play *To Kill a Mocking Bird*.

He is a Life member of the NAACP, Alpha Phi Alpha Fraternity, Inc., and the National Association of Black MBAs. He is also a member of the Athletic Hall of Fame, lettering in three sports at Alfred E. Beach High School in Savannah, GA. Charles is a Certified Management Consultant and a Fellow of the Institute of Management Consultants, Inc.

Charles E. Day, Sr. received his Bachelor of Science degree in mathematics, physics, and education from Savannah State University and Master of Science in administration and computer science from George Washington University in Washington, DC.

Printed in the United States
99996LV00004B/124-198/A